GAINING ACCESS

A Practical and Theoretical Guide
for Qualitative Researchers

MARTHA S. FELDMAN
JEANNINE BELL
MICHELE TRACY BERGER

ALTAMIRA PRESS
A Division of Rowman & Littlefield Publishers, Inc.
Walnut Creek • Lanham • New York • Oxford

ALTAMIRA
PRESS

ALTAMIRA PRESS
A Division of Rowman & Littlefield Publishers, Inc.
1630 North Main Street, #367
Walnut Creek, CA 94596
www.altamirapress.com

Rowman & Littlefield Publishers, Inc.
A Member of the Rowman & Littlefield Publishing Group
4501 Forbes Boulevard, Suite 200
Lanham, MD 20706

PO Box 317, Oxford, OX2 9RU, UK

Copyright © 2003 by AltaMira Press

British Library Cataloguing in Publication Information Available

Library of Congress Cataloging-in-Publication Data
Feldman, Martha S., 1953–
   Gaining access : a practical and theoretical guide for qualitative researchers / Martha Feldman, Jeannine Bell, and Michele Berger.
      p.   cm.
   Includes bibliographical references and index.
   ISBN 0-7591-0215-5 (cloth : alk. paper) — ISBN 0-7591-0216-3 (pbk. : alk. paper) 1. Social sciences—Field work. I. Bell, Jeannine, 1969– II. Berger, Michele, 1968– III. Title.
   H62 .F3915 2002
   300'.7'2—dc21   2002014164

Printed in the United States of America

CONTENTS

Introduction

PROBLEMS OF GAINING ACCESS often come as a rude surprise to the researcher who has developed a research design and is eager to get down to the important task of finding some answers. Access can seem like an obstacle only tangentially related to the actual research. Yet access is a critical part of doing research, not only because one must "get in" in order to gain information but also because the process of "getting in" affects what information is available to the researcher.[1] In this volume, we suggest thinking about access as a relational process and present access vignettes that illustrate the process.

This book both fills a theoretical void and brings together in a single work a diverse collection of access stories. We present a general theory of access that recognizes it as a process of building relationships. This process requires researchers to identify those who can help them gain access, to learn the art of self-presentation, and to nurture relationships once they are established. As part of this ongoing process, researchers must also deal with both rejections and the end of relationships. In sum, we utilize a relational perspective in understanding the fundamental nature of access.

Our vignettes show that being allowed to hang out in a particular setting to observe or being allowed to interview informants is just the first step of gaining access. Access, from our perspective, requires being in a position to learn from the people you are talking with and observing. From this perspective, access is not something that is gained once and for all but a process that can be developed and enriched over time. In part I, we discuss this process by breaking it down into several stages. In part II, we present a variety of access stories that illustrate this process. They specifically address not only how the researcher gained initial access but also how he or she built rapport with respondents. They also address the seldom-discussed issue of one's exit.

In this introduction, we first give an overview of our relational perspective. Then, we discuss the organization of the book.

The Access Paradox

Despite the importance of "getting in," the literature on qualitative methods has not yet provided an extended treatment of the issues of gaining access. Though many books and articles have sections on access or issues related to access, we have discovered only one book wholly devoted to the topic of access.[2] Much of the information on access is contained in appendices to specific studies.[3] The scattered nature of this literature means that researchers are often in the position of following the advice that Rosalie Wax articulated some years ago:

> The student who expects to be told precisely how to construct this kind of field relationship would do well to read a number of books. If he [sic] has the wit to be a good fieldworker, he will perceive how different were each of these situations and he may also understand why honest and experienced fieldworkers tell beginners that there is not much they can tell them, because each situation differs from every other.[4]

An even greater challenge is posed by the absence of theoretical models for thinking about access. Much that has been written about access has been presented in an ad hoc manner as a series of tips. Tips for getting access are important, but they are also peculiar to each situation.

The absence of a general theory of access may be related to the paradox of access. As a colleague recently described it, "We ask for so much and have so little to give."[5] The central paradox of access is that we have so little to offer our informants, *yet we still gain access.* In this regard there is much we do not understand with respect to the motivations of those being studied. For instance, several of our contributors describe people in the field who aided the researcher in the difficult task of gaining access. In facilitating access these individuals received little, if any, direct personal benefit. What prompted these people to help the researchers?

In this book, we illuminate the access paradox by viewing access through a relational lens. What motivates relationships in the research context is likely as diverse as what motivates relationships in any other context. People may help researchers because they achieve status through their connections with the researchers, because they see it as part of their job, because they see a vision of themselves at an earlier age or an image of what they might have become, or because they genuinely like the researcher and want her or him to succeed. Perhaps they allow access because they wish to further knowledge in the way that a study of their institution can provide.

While the specific motivations are clearly important in any particular context, in this guide we focus less on particular motivations and more on viewing access as a relationship in which motivations play an important role. By viewing the access process through a relational lens, we connect this process to something in which we all engage on a regular basis. Though the ins and outs of relationships of all types are sometimes mysterious, most of us still engage in relationships; many of us do so quite successfully. The relational lens not only relates access to something we all know how to do but also focuses our attention on key aspects of the process that can help us make decisions about what actions to take.

Thinking about Access

What has been written about gaining access often likens the process to opening a door.[6] This image of access suggests that a door exists, that it is always in the same place, that the researcher can find it, and that access involves having the right key or the right combination that enables one to open the door. The door image is supported by the use of the term *"entry"* for access. Thinking about access in this way places a lot of emphasis on the actions of the researcher, including planning, developing skills, and selecting one's site well. All of these are clearly important, but they are not sufficient to understand the process of access.

Our experiences with access suggest that the door image is too simple. A second, more complex image starts with a long hallway with a multitude of doors. Some of the doors are open; some are closed. Some of the closed doors open periodically in response to a variety of different actions; others will only open if you say or do the right things. Some of the doors lead to rich environments where there is much to be learned; other doors lead to vast empty rooms that contain little of interest to the researcher. Some of the doors may open but lead to spaces behind the doors that do not provide further access. Doors that open sometimes close, occasionally for no discernable reason. Conversely, a door that was closed may open just enough to allow one to get one's foot inside. Not all doors are completely open or shut. There is a range of in-between.

The image of the door is insufficient in another way: It fails to acknowledge that there are people on the other side of doors permitting access. These doors do not just open or close of their own volition but must be opened by people. Moreover, the act of entering the door is hardly the end but just the beginning of access. Both our contributors and other scholars describe access as a process that has many aspects or stages rather than a single act.[7] Gaining access is not simply a matter of banging on a door and getting it to open. "[A]ccess like research itself is a dynamic process."[8] One researcher describes access as a series of antechambers, multiple thresholds in which there is no "inside" in which researchers can safely reside.[9] "Seeking access continues, throughout the whole study. . . . [T]here is no such felicitous moment when the study can continue without hindrance."[10]

    To gain initial access, one must attract enough attention so that someone on the inside will look out the door and see who or what is there. It also requires that the researcher convince the person or people on the other side of the door to open it wide enough to explain why he or she wants in. The researcher must be invited in and be allowed to stay for a while. Leaving and returning are also parts to this process. Throughout this entire process, to be successful we must build relationships with people.[11] Gaining access is thus a relational process.

Access as Relational

The relational perspective can help researchers think about how to go about gaining access. Seeing access as relational moves us beyond the image of the door or single threshold that is either crossed or not. In conducting research, it is often necessary for the researcher to talk with many people, and thus to develop rapport with them, to be in a position to learn from them.[12] Access is thus a continuous and dynamic process. There is no point at which access is stable, though it may change more or less quickly. Seeing access as relational allows us to see that building rapport with individuals is as much a part of access as the initial contact and that the access process continues throughout and sometimes beyond one's exit from the field.

    While the relationships one develops in the field are different in many ways from other relationships, they have in common with other relationships the ongoing effort required to maintain and deepen them.[13] These relationships often require subtle negotiation at different points in the access process: initial contact, the rapport-building stage, and exit.

    Seeing access as relational also makes clear that control of the relationship is not entirely in the hands of either the researcher or the researched. Because of choices that confront *both* the researcher and the people from whom he or she wants to learn, the relationship can develop in many different directions, ranging from mere toleration to true friendship. People from whom the researcher wants to learn may resist having any relationship at all, or they may welcome the researcher with open arms.

    Different relationships may affect the research in different ways. People may help in ways that are different from those that the researcher intended and sought. They may suggest others from whom the researcher can learn. They may unintentionally tell the researcher much about the context about which the researcher is trying to learn. While the researcher does not have total control over these interactions, it is up to the researcher to turn whatever he or she can into an opportunity for learning.

    Seeing access as relational also emphasizes that identity matters. Who you are and how you present yourself influence access.[14] This makes sense from a relational perspective. Identity influences one's ability to relate to others, because of both their and your cultural understandings about identity.[15] Researchers draw on various aspects of their identity to create connections with other people. Being a scholar is often an important part of a researcher's identity and one that researchers tend to emphasize while conducting research. It is often valuable for researchers to do this because learning more about the reason for conducting the research is helpful for those who grant access.

One's identity as a researcher is not the only identity we have that can facilitate access. Some of these identities, which the researcher can reveal when it is likely to be helpful, include one's previous profession, geographic affiliation, political ideology, and hobbies or other interests. Other identities, such as gender, race, and age, will generally be apparent whenever there is face-to-face interaction. As we explain later in the book, while similarity in identity can facilitate the building of rapport, differences may be useful at drawing out explanations. A relational perspective helps researchers think about how their identities are affecting the likelihood that they will receive information as well as their ability to understand the information they receive.

Seeing access as relational emphasizes the importance of relationship-building skills in gaining access. One's ability to relate to others becomes a part of the research process.[16] Some people are better at having conversations or at keeping commitments. Some excel at keeping confidences. Some are better at conveying appreciation. Overall, a variety of interpersonal skills is important to developing and sustaining the wide range of relationships a researcher encounters during the process of gaining access.

Related to relationship-building skills is one's ability to be flexible, to be persistent without being annoying, and to recognize luck and accept opportunities when they are offered. The importance of these qualities and of the talent in using them appropriately and consistently are highlighted in the access stories. They are vitally important to the process. Flexibility and persistence appear at every stage of the access process. Luck often emerges in the confluence of initial encounters, chance meetings, and the ferreting out of new contacts in the first two stages of the access process. Luck, of course, continues to play a role during other stages of the access process, but its role is usually less relevant in "deepening" access as the researcher develops rapport with informants.

Organization of this Book

Part I of the book develops an understanding of the process of access as relational and continuous, while part II illustrates it through the stories of researchers gaining access in various settings.

Part I

In part I, we provide an overview of the access process. We divide this part into five chapters that correspond to stages of access. Chapter 1 examines the process of finding the people with whom you want to have a relationship. One could think of this stage as the attraction. Here we focus on the preparation for seeking access, the ways in which the researcher chooses to represent his or her research and the contacts and resources that are useful at this early stage. Chapter 2 explores seeking permission for the relationship. Here we review the process of gaining approval, including institutional review board approval, to conduct research at a particular site. Chapter 3 is about making initial contact. In friendships, the analogous stage is asking to go out for coffee. Conversely, in love relationships this stage corresponds to asking for a date. Here we discuss the ways the researcher used the preparation that he or she did in the first stage to secure initial access to people or the organization(s) they wish to study. Developing rapport, or building the relationship, is the subject of chapter 4. Here we describe how a researcher might build the kind of relationship necessary for access to the information the researcher desires. Chapter 5 describes the process of exit or, to use a relational metaphor, changing the terms of a friendship or ending a love relationship. This last chapter in part I provides a discussion of some of the difficulties and issues surrounding one's exit from the research site.

At the end of the chapters in part I, we have included some helpful guidelines that are culled from various researchers' stories. The authors' names (in parenthetical comments at the end of each story) allow the reader to reference the story from which the tip was culled, later in the book.

Part II

In part II, we provide access stories from a variety of different research perspectives. We follow a tradition in fieldwork that gaining access is an individual pursuit that is different for every field site and every researcher. Thus, this book does not provide a blueprint for gaining access to any particular setting. Instead, we supply many ideas and strategies that others have used. We have done three things to simplify the task. First, we have provided numerous access stories in one place. Second, we have provided a theoretical framework based on viewing access as a relationship that helps make sense of things that take place during the research process. The two fit together. The stories provide more than the customary story about "getting in" or initial access. Third, we have provided pointers to other access stories and literature about access.

To obtain information about the process of gaining access, we have solicited reports from a diverse set of researchers who have engaged in a broad range of research projects involving fieldwork. Experienced researchers and as well as those conducting their first study will find value in these access stories. Both veteran researchers and graduate students have written vignettes for this book. Most of the access vignettes describe the researchers' first research projects in which they were responsible for gaining access. For many, these are their dissertation projects. Even some of the experienced researchers have chosen to write about their first access experiences. The first access experience is not always the smoothest, but it is one in which the researcher is very reflective. Few things are taken for granted. The researcher remembers each torturous step. Four of the researchers report on research they undertook in later stages of their careers.

Our contributors are men and women who come from several different racial and ethnic backgrounds. Their disciplinary backgrounds include training in architecture, business, education, law, natural resources, political science, public policy, psychology, and social work. At least nine of the contributors had spent several years in other careers. Before conducting their research, they worked in teaching, law, architecture, consulting, programming, and planning. Thus, our contributors are diverse in many ways. This is particularly useful for understanding the relationship between identity and access. The effect of any particular identity may vary in different contexts. Seeing how the various identities represented by these people affect the information they are able to obtain in the research setting can help readers think about how their own identities may influence their research experience.

Contexts of Vignettes

Some of the access vignettes are about doing research that involves studying people who have no shared organizational or institutional affiliation. These vignettes include research about Arab American immigrants, Bosnian ethnic minorities, Chinese cadres, and American sex workers. In each of these contexts, contributors describe how to cope with the special challenges of gaining access to unaffiliated individuals. These stories represent what we consider to be the essential access experience: connecting to individuals.

An organizational or institutional context sometimes provides additional resources or additional obstacles that factor in the access process. Many of the vignettes provided in part II take place in various organizational contexts. Some of the vignettes are about gaining access to several people in a single organization. This includes research conducted in a hospital, school, police department, government agencies, and private sector organizations. Other vignettes describe gaining access to people in similar organizational contexts. These include stories about doing research in several prisons or welfare offices. Other vignettes discuss doing research in a particular institutional setting, such as the chemical industry or within the clergy. These contexts provide a wide variety of examples of how researchers can use the organizational and institutional contexts to help them develop relationships with people in these contexts.

Table I.1 provides a quick guide to the context of the research projects, so that readers can find research that is most relevant to them. We caution against a too narrow interpretation of what is relevant, however. While researchers studying in different settings or those requiring different levels of access (i.e., interviews vs. participant observation) often have to deal with different issues, research designs that are dissimilar may share similar challenges for access. As the vignettes written by our contributors show, opportunities as well as obstacles can pop up in surprising places.

Table 1.1. Subject and Location of Study

Author(s)	Subject of Study	Type of Organization	Location of Study
Bell	Hate crime unit of police department	Public	United States
Berger	HIV-positive sex workers	NA	United States
Brooks	Computer firms	Private	United States
Daniel-Echols	Welfare to work offices	Private and nonprofit	United States
Enomoto	High school truancy	Public	United States
Feldman	Department of Energy	Public	United States
Garcia-Johnson	Chemical industry	Public, private, and nonprofit	Mexico and Brazil
Ginger	Bureau of Land Management	Public	United States
Jamal and Lin	Arab immigrants	NA	United States
Jelen	Clergy	Nonprofit	United States
Lin	Prisons	Public	United States
Manion	Retirement norms	NA	China
Miller-Adams and Myers	World Bank	Nonprofit	United States
Perlow	Software engineering firms	Private	China, Hungary, India
Pickering	Bosnian ethnic minorities	NA	Bosnia
Pratt	Amway	Private	United States
Sandfort	Welfare offices	Public	United States
Schermer	Automobile company architects	Private	United States
Wrzesniewski	Hospital cleaners	Nonprofit	United States

Organization of Vignettes

The vignettes in this book are organized into five chapters. There is a cumulative nature to the organization of the vignettes. Issues found in the first set of vignettes are also found in all of the vignettes. Each chapter layers on a different set of issues for the researcher to deal with. In each chapter introduction, we highlight the main issues pertaining to the type of access that the vignettes raise. Additionally, we draw on work by other researchers to provide an even broader base of knowledge for the reader.

We start with what we think of as the quintessential issue of access: connecting to individuals. In the first four stories, the informants are not tied by a common organizational context. The issues raised in chapter 6 are found in all of the research, though sometimes altered by an organizational context in which the story takes place. In chapters 7 through 10, we include stories in which contributors sought access for interviewing, interviewing plus observation, extended observation, and finally for participation or membership.

All of the vignettes are ultimately success stories, though many recount setbacks experienced along the way. We think this is representative. While there are research projects that never get off the ground, our vignettes illustrate that gaining access often requires persistence and flexibility. Most of our researchers made substantial changes in their original research designs. The discussion of research design has been kept to a minimum in the vignettes. As a result, it may appear that the research designs of these researchers relied heavily on convenience and snowball techniques. In fact, the research designs were vetted both theoretically and methodologically. As mentioned earlier, many of the research projects discussed here were dissertation projects, and the research designs were given a great deal of scrutiny by dissertation committees before the students were allowed to attempt access. Thus, the vignettes show not a set of lax research designs but what the process of access does to research designs. In many cases, the access process forced researchers to decide what was really important to them and to be flexible on everything else. From this perspective, gaining access is a useful part of the research process, not only because researchers have to gain access to get the information they need but also because the process of gaining access is a powerful way of focusing their attention.

Acknowledgments

The authors are grateful to participants in ICOS (1999) and the Qualitative Forum (2001) at the University of Michigan and participants at the Western Political Science Association Meetings (2000) in San Jose for their comments and for the opportunity to present our ideas at early stages of development. We are also grateful to Peregine Shea-Schwartz for reading early copies of the manuscript and to Jane Dutton and Michael Cohen for helpful comments. We are particularly grateful to the authors who have contributed their access stories and to all of the people who have allowed us to learn from them.

Notes

1. Colin Brown, Pierre Guillet de Monthoux, and Arthur McCullough, *The Access-Casebook* (Stockholm: Teknisk Högskoletitteratur i Stockholm AB, 1976).

2. Brown et al., *The Access-Casebook.*

3. For a well-known example from political science that discusses in detail the author's attempts to gain access and develop rapport, see Richard Fenno, "Appendix: Notes on Method: Participant Observation," in *Homestyle: House Members and Their Districts* (Boston: Little, Brown, 1978). For an example that discusses the author's attempts to gain access to institutions at some length, see John DiIulio Jr., "Appendix: Prison Research," in *Governing Prisons: A Comparative Study of Correctional Management* (New York: Free Press, 1987).

4. Rosalie Wax, *Doing Fieldwork: Warnings and Advice* (Chicago: University of Chicago Press, 1973), 20.

5. Personal communication between Martha Feldman and Wanda Orlikowski, May 2001.

6. See Brown et al., *The Access-Casebook;* and Martin Hammersley and Paul Atkinson, *Ethnography: Principles in Practice* (New York: Routledge, 1992).

7. See Corrine Glesne and Alan Peshkin, *Becoming Qualitative Researchers* (White Plains, N.Y.: Longman, 1992), and J. A. Maxwell, *Qualitative Research Design: An Interactive Research Approach* (Thousand Oaks, Calif.: Sage, 1996).

8. Brown et al., *The Access-Casebook,* 34.

9. Barbara Czarniawska, *A Narrative Approach to Organization Studies* (Thousand Oaks, Calif.: Sage, 1998), 34.

10. Czarniawska, *A Narrative Approach,* 33.

11. Glesne and Peshkin, *Becoming Qualitative Researchers.*

12. See John Lofland and Lyn Lofland, *Analyzing Social Settings* (Belmont, Calif.: Wadsworth, 1995), 53–65; and James Spradley, *The Ethnographic Interview* (Fort Worth, Tex.: Holt, Rinehart & Winston, 1979), 78–83.

13. Maxwell, *Qualitative Research Design,* 66–69.

14. Brooke Harrington, "The Access Problem: Toward a Theory of Field Research Methods," unpublished manuscript, Brown University, 1999.

15. Spradley, *The Ethnographic Interview,* 44–45.

16. Spradley, *The Ethnographic Interview,* 45.

STAGES OF ACCESS I

Finding Informants   I

ESEARCH PROJECTS that involve obtaining information from people require researchers to think about from whom they want to gain information and how to appeal to these people. Whether one seeks a stratified random sample of anonymous survey responses or wishes to spend several months as a participant observer, it is necessary to think about how to find these. Some research can be conducted by sending questionnaires through the mail and hoping for a sufficient response rate. For other research, it is often necessary to determine whether one will have access before going ahead with the research. Regardless, it makes sense to find out as much as one can about what will make the people you want to learn from more likely to provide access.

Research projects often begin with the researcher's desire to understand a specific system, organization, or set of people. If the researcher can use data that have already been gathered about the system, organization, or set of people, then the researcher need only be concerned with gaining access to the data set. If the data are publicly available, access may be a straightforward process. If the data belong to another researcher, access may be more complicated. For researchers who need to gather their own data, gaining access may be further complicated.

Researchers who gather their own data, and particularly those who require data that takes a fair amount of the informant's time, need to find people who are willing to commit that time. For some researchers, gaining access is a process started anew for each person. For others, gaining access means finding an organization that will allow one to do research within it. Endorsement by management, however, can have diverse effects. In some cases, it encourages people within the organization to open their doors. In other cases, the endorsement will simply provide access to doors, and the researcher must still persuade the people on the other side to open them and to provide useful information. In still other cases, endorsement by management can close doors. Thus, even for those who do research within an organizational context, gaining access is a process that involves individual researchers developing relationships with individual informants.

Research Design and Access

Research design and access issues are integrally related. *Research design* involves how you decide who should be your informants and whether you have the right ones, while *access* involves convincing the people you have decided should be your informants actually to give you information. Stated as such, it appears that research design is prior to access and access is the execution of choices made in the research design. This is straightforward enough in theory. In practice, the relationship is often more complex.

First, scholars often design research with access in mind. There is, after all, little point in designing research that can never be fulfilled. Sometimes researchers design research around the access they have. One of our contributors, for instance, was involved in certifying a school and decided to use that site for her research. Others had a type of research setting in mind, tried to come as close as possible to what they envisioned, and altered their research designs as they discovered what access was possible. While these two approaches are different initially, after the initial access is gained, they look quite similar.

Access also alters research designs after the fact. Access often determines what information you have and therefore what questions you can answer. On the face of it, this statement appears to be negative, implying that people pull back from the questions they *really* want to answer because of lack of access. Undoubtedly, this sometimes happens. Often, however, researchers gain more access and thus more knowledge than they ever imagined they would have. Many of our contributors, particularly those who developed very rich relationships, answered questions in their research that they did not even know to ask before they had access.

When designing research, gaining access to individuals and organizations may seem formidable to some researchers, causing researchers to set their questions in a way that can be answered by data that are more easily available. For researchers who are determined to gather their own data, however, the act of pursuing access can broaden their project, their research design, and the questions their research ultimately answers.

One of our contributors changed the design of her study when she began to investigate field conditions in preparation for a study of local organizations in the state welfare bureaucracy. After spending time in local offices, she realized that the study would have more policy relevance were she to examine both public and private welfare-to-work contractors and changed her design. Another contributor had planned to study only a single group of architects involved in auto industry work because he was hesitant to ask for permission to enter sites, but he became more comfortable and ended up conducting on-site field research at an automobile company. Still another contributor exploring the transnational diffusion of international environmental ideology realized as she learned more about the diffusion process that she would have to interview not only the leaders of multinational corporations but also scholars, government policy makers and enforcers, and environmental activists. The research design was broadened to include these individuals. In each case, the researcher was able to answer broader questions as a result of having pursued access.

Beginning Preparatory Work

We call the first step in the process of pursing access "finding the informants." Using the romantic relationship as metaphor for this process, this first stage is a bit like attending a singles gathering in which one is attempting to see who is available and to signal one's own availability. Seeking access at this state is different from the initial search one is doing in romantic relationships, because in access, the searching is mostly one-sided. People are rarely looking to be informants, though they often enjoy it once the relationship is established. The metaphor is also apt in that this stage of access involves gaining as much information as possible about the potential informants, all the while trying to look appealing in case they glance your way.

This first thing you need to consider in this stage is where you will look for informants. Then, once you find them, how will you get to know them? Many people begin this process by doing some type of preparatory work that involves gathering information about the people and the setting from which they want to learn. This may involve reading up on the literature, obtaining the names and addresses of particular sites, or otherwise becoming familiar with the context in order to appear competent to those from whom they are requesting access. For several of our contributors conducting research abroad, this work included developing language skills and knowledge of another culture.

An understanding gained about the research site or the people to whom one wants to gain access is also often useful for the research itself. The knowledge gained at this point provides a context for interpreting knowledge gained later. Thus, access is not something that happens before and outside the research but is part of the research process.[1]

While the homework stage is important, the researcher should take care not to get stuck in it. It is easy to do this, for researchers often feel most in control during this part of gaining access. This is understandable given that some of preparatory work—reading articles and doing other background work—are extensions of the types of activities researchers do in other contexts and therefore find familiar. Researchers' comfort in this stage can lead them to prolong it beyond its usefulness. Access is hardly ever gained without going out and making contact with people. Preparation can also be overdone. As one of our contributors commented, it is important to be knowledgeable enough to be taken seriously, but not so knowledgeable that you think you already know the answers to your questions.

Contacting People

For several contributors, part of the preparatory learning process involved gathering information from the different individuals or research sites in person. For most of our contributors, this stage involved some form of making appointments with people and talking with them. These people may be gatekeepers, or they may be potential informants themselves. Some people serve dual roles, as when a researcher talks with the manager of an organization. The researcher may want access both to the manager and to the employees to whom the manager can provide access.

In addition of providing information useful to access, initial interviews may help better situate the researcher for access. For instance, two of the contributors' research interviews enabled them to gain access as participants. Given the potential of these initial interviews, it is important that the researcher approach these encounters in a way that shows one to be reliable, trustworthy, and open to all the site has to offer.[2] For instance, one might stress that one is interested in what happens and how, not whether something is good or bad, right or wrong.

For some contributors, part of their preparatory work involved making *cold calls*, in which the researcher making the call was unknown to the person he or she was calling. Though this approach could be difficult, because being unknown to members of the organization meant they had little incentive to speak with the researcher, contact with the organization was a critical part of the process. Not only do cold calls have the potential to provide information about the procedures for getting in and information regarding the type of site, but they can also supply data regarding the perspectives and norms of those inside. Understanding these perspectives and norms can be helpful in honing one's requests for access.

Developing Contacts

Developing contacts is often an important part of preparation. The networks that provide these contacts may have been developed over a number of years. Some of our contributors drew on networks from their graduate and undergraduate schools; others drew on networks they had developed in earlier work, in either paid or voluntary positions. Contacts from preexisting networks provided our contributors with varying degrees of assistance in the access process. One of our contributors, who had no contacts in the industry she planned to study, describes how she started to develop a list of potential informants:

> I had to network to develop a list of contacts. I visited professors at my graduate and undergraduate institutions, sent e-mail messages to Brazilian and Mexican student groups, and recorded the names and numbers of alumni from my universities in Brazil and Mexico. One professor provided the name of just one business executive, who in turn gave me the names and numbers of his colleagues working in company subsidiaries in Brazil and Mexico. I called these two individuals from the United States and made appointments to interview them when I arrived. These were the only appointments I had before I left the United States for my initial pilot work and fieldwork. (Garcia-Johnson)

Initial contacts may provide a wealth of assistance that ranges from information to entry into important networks.[3] Contacts may provide crucial information about the institution that the researcher can use to approach the site. In some cases, our contributors' initial contact gave a name of someone else who could guarantee access. Sometimes the help given by contacts was more indirect. The research arm of an organization one contributor wished to study provided help in writing a research proposal for which access would be more likely.

Identity

Identity is less a factor in the process of identifying and finding informants than in other stages in the access process. In this early stage, researchers tend to have a vague sense about how identity will impact their research. Their primary concern is usually with appearing competent and being taken seriously. Preparatory work can be important not only for figuring out who the researcher may want to approach but also for creating the identity of a serious researcher. This is the time when researchers prepare to present themselves to the people they want to learn from. Being able to articulate why these people are interesting and what the researcher has to learn from them is an important part of being ready to make initial contact.

Appearing competent can overlap with aspects of identity that will be evident when the researcher is face to face with potential informants. Age and gender, in particular being young and being female, may require extra effort in many settings to convince potential informants that they should take the researcher seriously. As we shall see later, however, appearing competent is just the beginning. Appearing trustworthy soon becomes much more important, and some qualities that are obstacles at one stage are advantages at another.

Persistence, Flexibility, and Luck

Several of our contributors looked in many places before finding the site that worked for their study. There are several reasons for this. One is that sometimes it takes a while to figure out *which* individuals can teach you what you want to know. This is true in part because researchers do not always know what information they need, and they do not always know where the information they want resides. Thus, one of our contributors wanted to study "communities of practice" in the automobile industry. At first, he assumed that what he needed was access to one of the big three automobile companies. He tried one company and then another. He felt that he was not gaining access. Finally, when he tried the third and did gain access, he found that it was probably more accurate to say that what he was looking for did not exist at the other places. In this case, therefore, it was not that the people at the other companies denied him access but that the people he needed to learn from were not there. One gets the sense from his account that the doors remained firmly shut at the other two sites because the firms were not organized in a way that would have allowed his research to make sense.

A second reason for persistence at this point is that there may be many possible research sites, and you need to knock on doors until some of them open. This was true for most of our contributors. Most of our contributors wanted to study particular types of organizations, such as welfare offices, police departments, or software engineering firms. They had no particular reason to study an exact site. Of a variety of sites or people, the researcher would have been happy with any site that allowed access. Similarly, the contributors who studied individuals such as Bosnian ethnic minorities or Chinese postrevolutionary bureaucrats did not need access to any particular person. One of our contributors wanted to study software engineers outside the United States and focused at first on Japan and Germany, but it turned out that the specific countries did not matter as much as the contrast between countries. Thus, many countries were possible sites. She ended up conducting her study in China, Hungary, and India.

For these researchers, finding the right people to learn from was largely an issue of finding people who were willing and ready to teach. Many of the potential informants were averse to being studied or simply saw no compelling reason to get involved. There are many reasons why potential informants may not want to be studied. Take, for instance, studying a police department. Bell found that a police department that has recently been involved in a scandal, that is getting used to a new chief, or that is in a tight budget period may not open its doors to researchers for a variety of reasons. One reason may be that the people in the organization are worried about the motives of the researcher or because they do not feel sure of themselves yet or because they do not feel that they have any resources to spare. These very real obstacles to access do, of course, affect what the researcher is able to learn. Does it matter that Bell's study of a hate crime unit in a police department took place in one city rather than another? It certainly matters in the sense that the particular context of hate in any city will affect the operation of the hate crime unit. But do we learn less because the study took place in a context in which people accepted Bell's presence? Though there are surely some things that cannot be learned in such a context, this context made people much more likely to talk openly with her and therefore made it possible for her to learn more about the complexities of a hate crime unit in general.

Finding the people who are ready and willing to teach involves great persistence. Researchers may have to make many overtures and be rejected many times. Asking again may take, as it did several of our contributors, several months. For instance, two of our contributors quickly gained access at one site, but their research designs called for a multicase study, and it took months for them to gain access to other sites. Bell's initial exploration of access to the police resulted in less than the full level of access she requested. Because this would have led to a drastic change in her research plan, she chose to pursue access at other sites.

Trying different sites also requires flexibility. At first we may be convinced that a particular site is the perfect place for the study we have designed. But often researchers have to rethink this notion when they find that access to the place or people they have targeted is not forthcoming. The questions then become, "What information do I need to gather, and who can help me acquire it?" Often the answers to these questions become apparent in the field, when one learns more about the data. One of our contributors who studied the World Bank, for instance, found gaining access to the most senior managers was not as valuable as he had initially thought. In his interviews, he discovered that senior managers did not always provide the most information. Sometimes it was those in more obscure offices who proved most helpful. Another contributor found her first site an especially rich one and decided to abandon her multisite study in favor of an in-depth single-case study.

Luck was also an important part of gaining access. Our contributors found that luck involved preparedness meeting opportunity. For many, luck came only after persistence and often required flexibility. In a number of vignettes, the researchers had all been working at gaining access for months when suddenly something happened that provided the access they needed. For instance, one contributor's big break involved a chance encounter in the subway with someone whom she had interviewed earlier. For her, like others, luck depended on work that had already been completed in an effort to gain access. Thus, luck has this funny quality: You cannot make it happen, but it does not happen if you sit around and wait. You have to do things that put you in a position to experience luck. Then you have to be willing to make the most of the opportunity.

Luck often involves meeting the right person, a person who can help open the doors that you need to go through. This kind of apparently selfless help does not happen every time, but it is not uncommon. An exchange-theory approach to human relationships may lead us to think that we must always give something to get something in return. But in this context, it is not always clear what the researcher is giving or, indeed, whether he or she is giving anything at all. It can be difficult at times to realize that this is help that you should accept. When doors open for no apparent reason, researchers may be wary and may even pass up valuable opportunities. Passing up an opportunity because one cannot figure out the motivations of those who have opened the door may prove to be a costly mistake. Many researchers have found that accepting the kindness of strangers is an important part of the research process.

Helpful Hints

We have listed here some of the helpful hints relevant to this stage of the access that are suggested in the stories in part II. Some of these have been discussed earlier; others have not. We have placed the name of the author in parentheses for easy reference.

- Gather information about the topic/organization you study—enough to show that you are serious and should be taken seriously (Garcia-Johnson).
- Ask for help, even from people who have no apparent reason to help you, and ask early (Lin).
- Talk to everyone—anyone might be a source of access (Perlow, Lin, Garcia-Johnson).
- Use networks (Lin, Garcia-Johnson).
- Learn the local language and culture (Garcia-Johnson, Jamal and Lin, Manion).
- Think about how the research might make sense to the people you are gaining access from rather than the sense it makes in the academic literature (Sandfort).
- Separate funding from access (Perlow).
- Persevere—repeat contacts (Sandfort) and try different contacts (Perlow).

Notes

1. Martin Hammersley and Paul Atkinson, *Ethnography: Principles in Practice* (New York: Routledge, 1992), 54–76.

2. Colin Brown, Pierre Guillet de Monthoux, and Arthur McCullough, The Access-Casebook (Stockholm: Teknisk Högskoletitteratur i Stockholm AB, 1976), 14*ff.*

3. See Robert Prus, "Sociologist as Hustler: The Dynamics of Acquiring Information," in *Fieldwork Experience Qualitative Approaches to Social Research,* ed. William B. Shaffir, Robert A. Stebbins, and Allan Turowetz (New York: St. Martin's, 1980), 135.

Human Subjects and Permission to Contact Informants

2

U NTIL RELATIVELY RECENTLY, the treatment of human subjects was generally a matter of personal and professional ethics and relied much on the discretion of the researcher.[1] Researchers needed to gain permission to conduct research from their informants and, sometimes, from an institutional gatekeeper. Scandals in both biomedical research and social science research, however, have led to the institution of various guidelines for ensuring the ethical treatment of human subjects.[2] The ethical treatment of human subjects has been institutionalized in some countries more than in others.[3] The United States and Canada both have extensive institutional processes for reviewing both biomedical and social science research.[4] In this chapter, we focus on the process that has developed in the United States.

We recognize that some readers of this text may not at first find this focus relevant. Some readers will not be subject to the permission process required in the United States. Some readers will find that their studies require permission from other institutional actors. These readers may yet find much relevance in this chapter. First, even researchers who are not required to obtain official permission may find that the ethical principles and the particular ideas for carrying them out are useful for their research. Those who have to receive other (perhaps additional) kinds of permission will find that many of the advantages and challenges of the permission process we focus on in this chapter are relevant to other permission processes. Understanding how these reviews work and the effects they have on research may be usefully generalized to a variety of contexts.

History

"The 'Modern' era of human subjects protection is routinely dated from the promulgation of the Nuremberg code in 1947."[5] This code, used as a standard of judgment in the Nuremberg doctors trial, established the idea of informed consent as a central feature of experiments involving human subjects. This idea has been further refined through the Declaration of Helsinki in 1964 and the International Ethics Guidelines for Biomedical Research involving Human Subjects, published by the Council for the International Organization of Medical Sciences in 1982. While much of the focus on ethical treatment of human subjects has been on biomedical experiments, studies such as the Milgram Study and Project Camelot[6] have focused attention on the harm that can be caused by social science studies.

In the United States, this concern about the mistreatment of human subjects has developed into a process that affects all research conducted by people who belong to organizations that receive funding from the federal government.[7] This process is overseen at the federal level by the Office of Human Subjects Research in the National Institutes of Health.[8] Research organizations such as universities are required to have institutional review boards (IRBs) that carry out the reviews of individual researchers' plans for interacting with human subjects. Institutional review boards are the mechanisms that have been established to implement the ethical principles contained in the Belmont Report, the work of the National Commission for the Protection of Human Subjects of Biomedical and Behavioral Research, created in 1974. The Belmont Report enunciated three basic ethical principles: respect for persons, beneficence, and justice.[9] Informed consent is an important means of fulfilling these three principles.

The reviews required by these institutional review boards are a significant factor in the pursuit of fieldwork by researchers in the United States. While specific questions vary from one review board to another, researchers in general need to submit descriptions of the research including the specific interactions with human subjects, such as interview questions or the kinds of observations or interventions the researchers will make. The researcher needs to answer questions regarding the kind of risk to those involved in the research and the efforts the researcher will make to protect them. The researcher also needs to explain how she will deal with informed-consent, which usually involves providing an informed-consent form that the informant will need to sign.

Complying with federal guidelines is a process that can be challenging for both new and established researchers. One might think that, at best, IRB approval is something that takes time but does not affect the course of the research, that it is another step that researchers have to go through before they can start their research. In 20 percent of the cases, the research is approved without any changes.[10] Yet even in these cases, it is possible that the IRB process has had an influence on the research design. Simply knowing that you have to submit the proposal can make people think more deeply about what they are proposing. In some cases, this thinking may inhibit the research in ways that are not constructive; but in other instances, this process may make the research better. In the following section we discuss some of the advantages of going through the IRB review.

The Advantages of the IRB Process

While many researchers experience difficulty with IRB reviews, this process also has advantages. It is useful to think about this matter from a relational perspective. First, the kinds of safeguards that a review board demands can help the researcher have a better relationship with the informants.[11] When researchers are concerned about the ethical aspects of their research, the informants feel more comfortable providing the information that the researchers seek.[12] As we point out in chapter 4, access is not just about being physically present but also about establishing trust and rapport with informants. Ultimately, the measure of access is the information that the researcher is able to obtain. If informants are not comfortable with the efforts the researcher makes to protect their security and their privacy, they may withhold or distort information.

Second, the reviews can help researchers think about aspects of the research that may raise difficulties for them later on. The ethical issues often arise in the writing process, long after the data have been gathered. At that point, researchers have developed a relationship with their informants and often feel personally bound not to expose them to any harm. Unfortunately, researchers may not know what could expose their informants to harm. An open discussion of what the informant is comfortable exposing—their names, their positions—may help researchers protect their informants.

Third, clearly defined consent forms and other forms indicating an understanding of the research and what the informant is agreeing to provide can make the research more secure for the researcher as well. When people are clear about what they are getting into, they seem less likely to renege on the commitment. While researchers may be tempted to go with "a bird in the hand," the long-term interest of the research may be better served by informants who are committed to the research process. One of our contributors found this out when she inadvertently gained access through a person who did not have authority to grant access. When she was denied access later, she discovered that she had invested lots of time in studying a site that was closed off and useless to her.

A fourth advantage to the IRB approval process is the protection it potentially provides to the researcher. The existence of the IRB process makes it possible for complaints about the research to be handled directly by the IRB office and, if necessary, by the legal staff of the organization. The IRB approval increases the ability of these professionals to deal with the complaints. If the research does not have IRB approval, these resources are unlikely to be available to protect the researcher.

The Challenges of IRB Approval

In addition to having some advantages, IRB approval certainly presents some challenges for researchers. In fact, horror stories abound about IRB approval. There is no doubt that the requirement that researchers seek IRB approval significantly adds to an already difficult process. One roadblock that researchers have faced is the requirement that they change their designs to satisfy IRB approval committees. One study prepared for the National Institutes of Health in 1998 found while only a few projects were rejected outright by IRBs, fewer than 20 percent of projects were approved as submitted.[13] This number will, of course, vary from one place to another and may vary by discipline. An IRB administrator at the University of Michigan, for instance, estimates the number of approved-as-submitted proposals at approximately 30 percent.[14]

Some of the challenges are related to the newness of the IRB process. IRB boards are emerging institutions in the research scene.[15] There is a great deal of variation over time. What projects need IRB approval as well as what is necessary for IRB approval is something of a moving target. An IRB administrator explains this variation in the following way:

> Although the regulations do get tweaked and changed occasionally, what happens more often is that, nationally, we interpret those regulations differently. For example, at one point in time we didn't really pay much attention to whether a phone number (contact person) was listed on the consent form. Then, there was more movement toward providing the subject with a copy of the consent form in case they had questions. Ultimately, it occurred to IRBs that the consent is not very useful if there's no contact information on it for them to call the investigator for either questions or a rescheduling of appointments. And now, the newest "suggested action" is to include the IRB information for anyone who has questions about their rights as a research subject. We continue to evolve.[16]

While there is some communication between IRB administrators in different organizations, this evolutionary process necessarily results in variation from one board to another. Variation over time and place inhibits the development of standard practices for researchers.

The following experiences suggest some of the challenges posed by current IRB reviews. Take, for instance, the experience of one of the authors of this book. She was conducting a study involving very public processes conducted by city administrations. The study was a multiyear study and had been approved twice (in 1998 and 1999) as the researcher had submitted it. In 2000, the review board asked for clarification of a procedure that had been reviewed several times. The researcher provided the information requested and asked why the information had been requested. The IRB administrator told her that if the file had been pulled by an outside examiner, it would have raised concerns. In 2001, the review board asked for minor changes to the consent form—a form that the researcher had used for three years. The changes were unobjectionable, and the researcher made them and resubmitted the form. She waited for two weeks, and having heard nothing, she inquired about the delay. The administrator reported that the review board had asked for another change in the consent form. This time the change was not acceptable. The review board wanted interviewees to give blanket consent to have their identity revealed. The researcher has a policy of providing the text of any paper about to be published with a person's quotes and asking them if it was all right to use their name. As much meaning is given to a person's words both in how they are transcribed (e.g., where punctuation is added) and by how they are placed in a context, it did not make sense to the researcher to ask a person for such blanket approval. She raised this point with the administrator and then waited. Another week passed, and the administrator sent back a message that was entirely unclear. It said nothing about the phrase that was under question and asked for another change that had already been made. The researcher sent back another message requesting clarification and received nothing. About a week later, the researcher received approval. It was still not entirely clear what was being approved.

This story illustrates several points. As noted earlier, the standards for acceptable studies are evolving. The reference to an outside examiner is particularly important. Research organizations are subject to reviews of their reviews. All the research approved by a particular review board can be suspended if the review board procedures are deemed inadequate. This occurred in 2001 when a healthy person involved in a study at Johns Hopkins University died, and the Office of Human Research Protection suspended "virtually all human subjects research across the university—about 2,400 studies."[17] The reason offered was that the university had not provided careful review of the research protocols and that specific criticisms of the protocol in question had not been addressed. The university objected to both the suspension and the reasons given, but the power of the Office of Human Research Protection to suspend not only specific research but also all research approved by the IRB that had approved the offending research was clearly established. In light of this power, review boards are likely to be cautious in the future.

The story also illustrates the organizational features of the reviews. Differing disciplinary training or conventions may lead scholars to evaluate the risk and benefits of the research—one issue that IRBs must determine—differently.[18] What seemed completely reasonable to an earlier review board may not to the next one. IRB administrators also change. The institutional memory of review boards is likely to be dependent on the administrator. If there is turnover at both levels, understandings about the research may be lost entirely. Such turnover may result in rough transition periods during which the new participants iron out the processes for doing their work. New participants in the reviews may institute new procedures, which may have implications for the researchers. In the earlier instance, for example, when the researcher asked why the review was taking so long, she was told that reviews generally take three to five weeks. Before the new procedures were instituted, the reviews of research had taken one week or less. One of the contributors in our book was even able to get a twenty-four-hour turnaround a few years earlier.

Other organizational issues are relevant as well. IRB approval is subject to all of the vagaries of any other organizational process. Communication problems, work overload at certain times of the year, differences in the competence or knowledge of the people running the process, and problems achieving coordination among the members of the board or between the board and the administrator may all affect the review.

All of these issues are exacerbated for the researcher dealing with vulnerable populations, such as children, prison inmates, or individuals who are ill. Such studies are subject to more scrutiny by a larger group of reviewers, increasing the likelihood that someone will find something to which they object. Take the experience of a researcher who was studying cocaine distribution networks by interviewing people in prison:

> Getting permission to conduct my prison interviews was extremely time-consuming and difficult. The whole process took well over a year. In addition to the federal Bureau of Prisons, which reviewed my request at three different levels of bureaucracy (local, regional and national), I also had to get permission from the University . . . IRB. Because the Bureau of Prisons had already granted tentative approval by the time I approached the [university] IRB I didn't think that I would have a problem with the latter group. I was wrong.
>
> The [university] IRB was even more demanding, at times demonstrating considerable reticence to approve the project. Although the IRB raised valid concerns I also believe that they went a little overboard. Apparently, the [university] had caught some heat for a previous research project based on prison interviews and they were extremely concerned about my proposal. Also, the director of the IRB was a psychologist who expressed his disapproval of the poli sci/sociological orientation of my interview instrument (this came out during a face-to-face conversation). He also went so far as to suggest that my project was potentially dangerous because I was learning how to become a proficient drug trafficker. (I responded that my interest lay in studying organized crime not participating in it.)
>
> Every time I addressed a specific set of concerns raised by the IRB the director came back with another list of extremely unlikely situations/concerns emanating from the modifications. Finally, one of the other members of the IRB (a sociologist who studies organized crime) admitted that they were putting me

through the wringer and that it had gone too far. At their next meeting, largely based on this guy's input, the IRB approved my protocol.

When I finally conducted the interviews they all went beautifully and there were no problems whatsoever.[19]

Making the Process Easier

Institutional review boards often require concise statements about how you plan on protecting your subjects, the risks and benefits of the research to your informants, how you will handle sensitive data, and other issues. They often require a reasonable amount of thought about how to protect the privacy and security of the informants through the researcher's handling of the data pre- and postinterview.[20] The preparatory work a researcher engages in discussed in chapter 1 can help in this process. Being organized, starting early, and talking to peers—all of these are important. Talking to others who have gone through the institution's review board is most important. Such conversations can save a researcher time and energy. It is also important to start early because these procedures can take a very long time. Many of the contributors to this volume commented on this reality.

IRB approval for most of the studies described in this book was straightforward. There are several possible explanations. First, the majority of the studies in this volume did not involve the study of vulnerable populations. Those that did had a more prolonged approval processes.

Second, many of the studies in part II took place at a time when the purview of IRBs was less broad and the reviews were not taken as seriously. Over time, the IRB's purview has spread from research that is supported by federal funds to research that is intended for publication, to any research conducted by anyone associated with the university. Incidents in which all university research is stopped have also made clear the importance of the reviews to the health of the entire university community and have increased the intensity of the evaluations.

Third, many of the studies went through the IRB approval at the same institution. While not all researchers can take advantage of the first two reasons, this third reason does provide the researcher with some leverage. The leverage consists of a relational strategy. Over the years, researchers in this university have had much contact with the IRB administrator and committee members. Professors at the university make a conscious effort to build and maintain connections with the IRB administrators and to make clear that ethics plays an important role in the methods courses they teach. As a result, many of the issues that arise for people doing fieldwork have already been resolved in the minds of the IRB.

The strategy of connecting to an IRB and administrator suggests there is another layer to the relational aspects of gaining access: developing relationships with those who give permission to pursue the research. Developing these relationships can be a very important part of the access process not only for oneself but also for other researchers at your university. As with other relationships, this strategy must be repeated as IRBs and administrators change.

Making oneself available to meet with the IRB and ethics committee to address specific questions in person may also be part of the relational strategy. Sometimes a researcher who undertakes field research might not have all aspects of the project explicated and may find it difficult to frame the research through traditional hypotheses and outcomes (which tend to be more suited to quantitative, experimental, and clinical projects). Instead of not answering "proposed outcome" questions, one researcher's strategy consisted of writing a short letter to the IRB explaining the process of how she went about filling forms in trying to answer their questions: "I have found it useful to write to ethics committees and explain how I have filled in their forms and why I have done so, especially with respect to not being able to conceptualize certain details of the research fully until the study is actually underway."[21]

Persistence and flexibility are also assets in this part of the process. The fact that 80 percent of all proposals need revision before being approved suggests that being prepared to revise and compromise helps in this process. Our contributors have certainly found this. Thus, researchers need to submit their proposals substantially before they need approval. In addition, researchers should be prepared for criticism and should try to deal with the criticism as constructively as possible.

Helpful Hints

Listed here are some of the helpful hints relevant to this stage of the access process. Some of these have been discussed already; others have not.

- Assess what permissions are needed for your study and who needs to provide approval.
- If more than one approval is required, send the project simultaneously to all for review. Get clear guidelines about your responsibilities and restrictions from the IRB before you enter the field.
- Allow plenty of time for the permission process.
- If your study involves vulnerable populations, deception, or other elements of risk, allow extra time for approval. For IRB approval, such studies are likely to be reviewed by the full board.
- Send in as complete an application as possible.

- Gather information about the review process. Talk with people who have experience with the permission process you need to follow. Read information provided by the relevant review board. Some universities have online tutorials than can be very useful.[22]

Notes

1. A good discussion of ethical issues in fieldwork can be found in Murray Wax, "Some Issues and Sources on Ethics," in *Handbook on Ethical Issues in Anthropology*, ed. Joan Cassell and Sue-Ellen Jacobs (Arlington, Va.: American Anthropological Association, 1987).

2. Michael Agar, *The Professional Stranger: An Informal Introduction to Ethnography* (Orlando, Fla.: Academic Press, 1980), 54; Barber, "The Ethics of the Use of Human Subjects in Biomedical Research (The Prototype Case)," in *Effective Social Science: Eight Cases in Economics, Political Science, and Sociology*, ed. Bernard Barber (New York: Russell Sage Foundation, 1987); Cynthia McGuire Dunn and Gary Chadwick, *Protecting Study Volunteers in Research* (Boston: Center Watch, 1999), chap. I; Joan Sieber, *Planning Ethically Responsible Research* (Newbury Park, Calif.: Sage, 1992), 3–9.

3. Information on the international extent of human subjects reviews is not readily available. According to the Office of Human Research Protection (U.S. Department of Health and Human Services) website, eighty-nine countries are "on file" as international IRB organizations as of 14 March 2002: ohrp.osophs.dhhs.gov/humansubjects/assurance/fiorg.htm.

4. Information about the review process in Canada was available at the following website in 2002: www.nserc.ca/programs/ethics/english/policy.htm.

5. Dunn, *Protecting Study Volunteers*, 4.

6. Agar, *The Professional Stranger*, 55.

7. The federal policy that these rules are based on can be found at ohrp.osophs.dhhs.gov/humansubjects/guidance/45cfr46.htm.

8. The Office for Human Research Protections (OHRP) was formerly called Office for Protection from Research Risks. OHRP is organizationally located in the Department of Health and Human Services. OHRP is charged with interpreting and overseeing implementation of the regulations regarding the Protection of Human Subjects codified at title 45, part 46, of the Code of Federal Regulations (45 CFR 46) promulgated by the Department of Health and Human Services (DHHS). Also, OHRP is responsible for providing guidance on ethical issues in biomedical and behavioral research. A major difference between OHSR and the OHRP is that the OHSR's activities are limited to the Intramural Research Program (IRP), National Institutes of Health, while the OHRP has oversight and educational responsibilities wherever DHHS funds are used to conduct or support research involving human subjects. (Source: ohsr.od.nih.gov/whatohrp.php3.)

9. Sieber, *Planning Ethically Responsible Research*, 6–7; also available on the Internet in 2002 at ohsr.od.nih.gov/mpa/belmont.php3#xrespect.

10. "Protecting Human Beings," 56.

11. Sieber, *Planning Ethically Responsible Research*, chap. 4.

12. Sieber, *Planning Ethically Responsible Research*, chap. 4.

13. "Protecting Human Beings," 56.

14. Kate Keever, administrator of the Human Subjects Protection Office, University of Michigan, conversation with author, 15 February 2002.

15. We are grateful to Ronie Garcia-Johnson for this insight.

16. Kate Keever, administrator of the Human Subjects Protection Office, University of Michigan, e-mail communication with author, 18 February 2002.

17. "New IRB Tackles Re-reviews."

18. "New IRB Tackles Re-reviews," 61.

19. Michael Kenney, e-mail communication, July 10, 2001. To read the product of this research, see Michael Kenney, "Intelligence Games: A Comparative Analysis of the Intelligence Capabilities of the Drug Enforcement Agencies and Drug Trafficking Enterprises," *International Journal of Intelligence and Counter Intelligence* (Summer 2003), in press; and Michael Kenney, "When Organizations Out-Smart the State: Understanding the Learning Capacity of Colombian Drug Trafficking Organizations," *Transnational Organized Crime* 5, no. 1 (Spring 1999): 97–119.

20. Julianne Creek, "An Untold Story: Doing Funded Qualitative Research," in *Handbook of Qualitative Research*, ed. Norman K. Denzin and Yvonna S. Lincoln (Thousand Oaks, Calif.: Sage, 2001), 401–20.

21. Creek, "An Untold Story," 411.

22. If your university does not have a tutorial, try the one at the University of Michigan. In 2002, it could be reached through http://cgi.www.umich.edu/cgi-bin/genlogin?003&/~drda/index.html.

Making Initial Contact 3

THE PROCESS of finding the people you want to learn from sometimes overlaps with the process of gaining the attention of the intended organization or population. Nonetheless, we deal with this as a separate stage in the process because it often happens that even after finding the right people, making initial contact still requires much work. Success happens when researchers are able to convince their contacts of two main things. First, researchers need to help potential interviewees and informants see why they would want to spend their time finding out about the research. This involves having some way of attracting the attention of and appearing interesting to the people you want to learn from. Second, researchers need to allay the initial fears that their interviewees and informants might have about the research. To do this, researchers need to construct themselves as credible and trustworthy and their research as beneficial, or at least not harmful.

Initial Contact

Initial contact often takes place through a letter. The letter can be thought of as the opening step in a new relationship. The letter typically introduces the topic of the research and the researcher. It needs to give the recipient some motivation to consider opening the door for the researcher. If one has a contact whose name can provide an initial frame of reference, it is good to mention it early in the letter, as the contributor does in the letter cited later. It is very important that description of the research be succinct and efficiently convey why the sender is an appropriate person to be involved in the research. The letter also needs to present the identity of the researcher in a fashion that suggests that she or he is a serious researcher who will make good use of the time that the recipient can give to the research. Here, in less than one page, the letter explains the project and presents the researchers qualifications, both his degrees and his experience in the field.

The letter needs to deal with logistics. It should tell what kind of access the researcher would like and when the researcher will call to follow up. In the sample letter, the researcher indicates that he will contact the recipient's secretary within a few days. Researchers should not assume that the recipient will get back to the researcher. Several of our contributors reported having to make several follow-up calls to arrange in-person meetings. The letter may also discuss the kind of confidentiality measures being taken by the researcher and state whether the research has been (or is in the process of being) approved by the university's IRB. Confidentiality measures may put those granting access at ease and encourage the recipient to be more receptive to the researcher when he or she calls to follow up.

One of our contributors, Brian Schermer, used the protocol prescribed by Richard Bolles in his well-known job-hunting and career guide, *What Color Is Your Parachute?*[1] to establish initial contacts. The letter he wrote based on this protocol follows:

> Dear _____:
>
> I am writing to you at the suggestion of Bob Beckley, Dean of the College of Architecture and Urban Planning at the University of Michigan, and Bob Johnson, formerly of the U of M and now Director for the CRS Center for Leadership and Management in the Design and Construction Industry at Texas A&M University. Both send their regards to you.
>
> I am a Ph.D. candidate in architecture at the U of M, and I am currently conducting research on how large organizations manage their facilities design and construction programs. The goals of my research are to provide architectural educators with insights that will help them prepare future architects to better serve the needs of organization clients, as well as to provide organizations with insights about how to organize for design.
>
> I am writing to you because I want to learn more about the scope and nature of facilities design, construction, and management at General Motors. I would greatly appreciate the opportunity to meet with you for about an hour or so. I will contact you or your secretary in the next few days to set up a meeting time.
>
> My research on design management is being funded by a grant from the CRS Center and the Graduate School at the U of M. Prior to returning to school, I worked for over ten years as both an in-house and consulting architect to organizations, which are involved in extensive and ongoing design and construction programs. I have enclosed a copy of my résumé so that you can get a better sense of my background.
>
> Thank you very much for your attention.
>
> Sincerely,

The letter is a good opportunity to say why you are someone to be taken seriously. Specifying what you are interested in learning from a particular interviewee or why you want to interview that particular person is an important part of the initial approach. In our contributor Jelen's research on the clergy and also in our contributors Miller-Adams's and Myers's research on the World Bank is discussion of customizing letters and phone calls. Myers even included the names of papers written by intended interviewees articles that he had read and commented that he would like to inquire more deeply into the issues covered by these papers.

During initial interviews, it is also important to display your serious intent as a researcher. Sometimes this means showing your credentials, usually by explaining a little about what you do and why you are interested in interviewing this particular person. In some circumstances this requires showing that you have done your homework. Sometimes researchers find that the people they are interviewing test them. One contributor, for instance, was asked a couple of times to display his skills in "speaking Latin," apparently to show that he really was the Catholic he said he was.

In all circumstances, it is important to make clear that you are there to learn from the interviewee. Jelen discusses approaching the interview for what you can learn as an important aspect of access. In his research, he started out with some biases that made it very difficult for him to hear what people were saying to him. As he points out, he was fortunate that his interviewees called him on it and that he had these interviews early on in the research so that he could change his approach to the interviews and gain access to information that helped him understand his topic better.

Letters are not the only way to make initial contact, though they are probably the most common. In some instances, informants may not have addresses or may not want to give the researcher their addresses. One of our contributors studied sex workers and made contacts face to face. This was also true for our contributors who studied Bosnian ethnic minorities and Arab American immigrants. Clearly, not having an organizational locus for the study makes letters a less likely means of making initial contact, but our contributor who studied Chinese bureaucrats found letters a useful means of contact. Others who did have an organizational locus still found that they needed to make initial contact either over the phone or face to face. For some this was because letters would be too slow. One of our contributors interviewed people in Mexico and Brazil. She started with just a few names and developed a snowball sample[2] while she was in the country. She had only a limited time to complete her interviews and found that the telephone was the best way to start. Sometimes one needs to make a phone call or pay a visit to a field site to figure out whom to write a letter to. This may be considered preparatory work, but sometimes it turns out to be initial contact.

Developing a "Hook"

One of the key aspects of the initial contact, whether in a letter or another form, is what you say to potential informants, interviewees, and gatekeepers about your research. People often refer to this as "the hook." We believe that a hook is an example of a clever, resourceful, and malleable tool in the access process; it does not necessarily imply manipulation on the part of the researcher.

Researchers use two facets of the hook while in the field. First, a salient hook attracts initial attention and "hooks" it toward the researcher. Second, a hook is also a metaphor for the place on which organizations and individuals can "hang" their worries, fears, and concerns about the research. A well-crafted hook confirms to others that the researcher is competent and trustworthy and that this relationship that they are entering into with the researcher is satisfactory. Gaining access is a negotiated process involving people and relationships. In the early stages of the research process, a hook assists in building these relationships.

Developing and executing a hook takes time, effort, and skill. The hook written in a letter or articulated verbally should minimally accomplish four things: (1) get someone's attention about how she can help the researcher achieve initial access, (2) briefly (and we mean briefly!) summarize the research project, (3) suggest why the researcher is a competent person to conduct the study, and (4) describe how this research will be beneficial to the organization or to the individual being studied. Research access is seldom granted without a developed hook. Even if a hook is not required for initial contact, somewhere in the access process a researcher will be asked and expected to justify his presence to others.

An explanation of the research project was included in the hook that each of our contributors used. This explanation, however, is not the only or always the most important part of the hook. For many of our contributors, referrals from friends, colleagues, or other people in the field served as their primary hook. People agreed to hear what they had to say about their project or even agreed to talk with them on the basis of their friends' or colleagues' recommendations. For one contributor, an important hook was renting a room in a family's apartment. The rent she paid contributed to the family's livelihood, and by living with them our contributor gained their trust.

Get Attention

Successful hooks draw the attention of the party from whom the researcher is requesting access. To do this, many of our contributors attempted to present their projects in a way that was the most interesting and most compelling to the particular audiences they were addressing. Different audiences have different interests and different resources for understanding one's proposal. For instance, one contributor who wanted personal, rather than professional, perspectives from retired Chinese bureaucrats explained her project by appealing to their vanity and common sense. Another contributor who was studying prisons had to appeal to multiple audiences—researchers and practitioners, prisoners, staff, and supervisors—in a single version of her proposal. She therefore tried to appeal to interests they had in common in order to gain their attention.

Like other stages of attempting to gain access, persistence and flexibility matter when trying to gain attention. One contributor who had a number of false starts before finally gaining access to computer companies described her problem as one of marketing. She noted that she essentially needed to combine her skills and research agenda into something that she could sell to the companies from whom she needed access. Solving the marketing problem, for this and other contributors, frequently involves conducting careful "market research," to discern the interests of those who one wishes to study.

Summarize the Project

At this point in face-to-face contact it is important for the researcher to have a succinct summary of the project. Think of your explanation in layers, with the big issues that appeal to a broad audience as the first layer and each layer successively more detailed and, perhaps, more academic. This makes it easy for people to understand why they should participate in your study and also enables people who want more information to get it easily.

For most contexts, you want to describe your interests in terms that appeal to people outside academia. It is useful to have a way of describing the research that is broad enough to appeal to many different people and yet narrow enough to be meaningful. One of our contributors, for instance, described her study as being about the role of information in decision making. The beauty of this description was that it tapped into common perceptions that information is important to decision making and that decision making is important. At the same time it allowed the researcher great latitude to investigate a wide variety of activities. Anyone who wanted more information about what the researcher would be doing could simply ask. A few people did, and she was ready with examples of what might be important. One example she used was whether it mattered who initiated information. People are generally not interested in the details of your study at this point. They need to hear something that makes sense to them, and they need to be assured that the researcher is serious and has thought about the work he or she is doing.

This ability to summarize the project would also include being as clear as possible about the time line of the research, any specific resources that the researcher might need, and what expectations the researcher and cooperating parties bring to the project. It is also useful at this point to be as clear as possible about the full level of access required. Some of our contributors were able to think in advance about the people, events, and things (e.g., records) that they wanted access to and the resources they would need. Others were unaware of either what they would want or what would be possible. In general, however, our contributors were clear about the level of access they desired even when they were not clear about the specifics. If they wanted to do extended observation or participation, for instance, that is the level of access they requested. This seemed to work well for our contributors. While anticipating the full extent of contact may be impossible, asking for a particular level or kind of access appears to make it easier to ask for access to specific events or situations later.

This advice may at first seem counterintuitive. From a relational perspective, asking for what you need immediately is a bit like telling people to be clear what they want from a friend when they first meet. Researchers, like anyone else starting a relationship, are apt to feel timid about pushing too hard at the beginning. They may even hope that asking for a little access will incline others to be more generous as time goes on. But an attempt to be cautious can backfire if those in the site feel that the researcher has misled them about the kind of access required.

One of our contributors experienced such a response firsthand when she tried to parlay one kind of access into another. It did not work well. She had a foot in the door doing temp work and then revealed that she actually wanted to do research observation. She was asked to clean out her desk at the end of the day and not return. This is an interesting example from the relational perspective. In one sense, she had a relationship with the organization where she wanted to do research. The position she had attained, however, was not a step in the process of gaining access to, and developing a research relationship with, the people inside the organization.

Establishing a good relationship in the field, however, can lead researchers to gain more access than they expected. Those who engaged in participation, particularly, found themselves more drawn into their research settings than they would ever have negotiated or been able to negotiate in advance. Even at less intense levels of access, many of our contributors received more access than they either asked for or were officially granted. For example, one contributor asked to be able to observe for twelve weeks. She was granted eight weeks but actually observed for more than five months.

Many of our contributors also asked for access to specific types of activities and resources. Based on their experience, we advise researchers to resist the urge to be reticent about asking for what they want when negotiating initial access. Identifying specific resources that will aid the researcher is particularly relevant for research that takes place in an organization. This is the time to ask for resources that seem reasonable, depending on the length of stay and type of access required to complete the project: a quiet, private room in which to interview people, a locker for materials, and a desk or file cabinet space (especially if the researcher is "hanging out").

It is also instructive for the researcher to get a sense of what is not going to be offered in this process (at least not initially), including privileges reserved for employees, parking stickers, keys, photocopying or fax privileges, and the like.

Legitimate the Researcher

It is often important, as part of gaining initial access to legitimate the researcher—to demonstrate to those from whom one is seeking access that the research is being conducted by a credible researcher who will behave in a professional manner. Professional identity is probably the most common way to legitimate the researcher. Our contributors used their institutional affiliations and their status as researchers (either established researchers or graduate students) to provide their potential informants and interviewees a sense of their scholarly intent. One contributor used his professional status at a Catholic institution to help facilitate his access to studying the political leadership of local clergy. One researcher utilized her graduate student status and her status as an employee of an accrediting organization to facilitate access to a high school that was being investigated because of its high incidence of truancy. For many, simply invoking the name of their universities was a useful way to draw on positive images of researchers. For some, of course, the university affiliation had to be downplayed, as the image of university researchers is not positive in all quarters.

Contributors also used earlier experiences, either with the organizations they were trying to enter or with related organizations. One contributor used her past work to convince people that not only would she understand what they were telling her but that she would also be able to contribute to the work they were doing. Another contributor drew on her past work with nongovernmental organizations (NGOs) and activists within these groups to indicate her serious concern for the people she interviewed. Other contributors used former professional identities to indicate both their knowledge of the work their informants were doing and to tap into a status structure that would convince those in the field that they should be taken seriously. For instance, a former architect and a former lawyer both emphasized their professional histories in their initial contacts.

Explain the Benefits

The benefits of the research are often difficult for the researcher to discern and articulate at the beginning of a project. It is important at the beginning not only to explain what the research is about but also to suggest reasons why an organization or population might benefit from helping a researcher. This is particularly important for populations that are vulnerable in some way. One of our contributors, for instance, studied ethnic minorities in Bosnia; another, HIV-positive sex workers using crack cocaine; another, the hate crime unit in a police department. As these groups are vulnerable to physical attack, stigmatization, and public scrutiny, it was particularly important for the researchers to identify ways in which their work might benefit the communities that they were studying. The earlier preparatory step of gathering information about the organization or individuals being studied helps the researcher formulate benefits relevant to the people or institutions being studied.

The benefits our contributors offered to the organizations and individuals they studied were many and diverse. The most common benefit they provided was to allow their informants to tell stories about their lives and work. The research they did offered at least the possibility of providing insight to the informants themselves or to audiences the informants cared about. The opportunity to talk and to have their vignettes heard was especially important because, many contributors reported, their informants felt misunderstood. This included a wide range of people, such as police officers, sex workers, executives in the chemical industry, people in peripheral offices of the World Bank, ethnic minorities in Bosnia, and people who clean hospitals. To these people our contributors offered a sympathetic ear. In addition, our contributors sometimes offered material support, such as rent, food, or transportation.

Talk to the People Who Can Grant Access

The transition from cold calling, letter writing, and holding informal meetings to meeting the appropriate people who can further assist with research access is usually the first chance the researcher has to develop the hook fully and see what works in the field. This is the time that not only "what you say" but also "whom you say it to" becomes paramount.

It is crucial that the researcher find the person or people who can grant initial access. It is not, however, always easy to figure out how to find the right person. Even in formal bureaucracies, it may not be clear who has the power to grant access.[3] In some organizational contexts, talking first to the most senior person in the organization who can grant access can be vitally important. However well one gets along with others lower down in the hierarchy, one's relationship with this person may be most indicative of how much access one will have or how long. This may be particularly true if the most senior person truly holds the key to one's access to the organization. One of our contributors interviewed one organization's second in command before she interviewed the program's actual director. Unfortunately, the relationship between the researcher and the director was not good, and the contributor's access privileges were withdrawn two weeks into her data collection.

Many contributors, however, never gained access from the top. For some the idea of the "top" is absurd. When doing research in the Department of Energy or Ford Motor Company, it does not make sense to get permission from the secretary of energy or from the CEO of Ford unless the research directly involves their offices. In such cases, the "top" is relative, and it may take the researcher a while to figure out who, if anyone, can grant access. Others found that gaining access from the top raised issues for the people whom they gained access to. One contributor, for instance, started at the top of the Bureau of Land Management and in successive summers worked her way down four levels of hierarchy. At each level, she was provided access from the level above. But she found that she had to deal with suspicions that the previous office was simply trying to get rid of someone who was incompetent or worse.

Gatekeepers

In some sense, all researchers have to gain access to each person whom they interview, observe, or use as an informant. Sometimes, however, people in organizations serve as gatekeepers to the employees or the clients or the organization. Gatekeepers can grant or deny initial access and make access either more or less difficult. Our contributors provide examples of both positive and negative experiences with gatekeepers, which we discuss briefly in this section. If there are no gatekeepers, then every individual is the person who can grant access. This means that with each introduction or at each door, you need to make the pitch again.

Access via a gatekeeper often makes research easier, as this person, in a sense, vouches for the legitimacy of the researcher to all the other people to whom one gains access. Thus, some of the work of the hook has to be accomplished only once. One group of contributors found this to be the case in their research on hospital workers. Early in their search for access, they found one person who was so supportive of their research that she resolved not only legitimacy issues but also logistical problems for them.

But gatekeepers can also be obstacles. One of our contributors studied women addicted to crack cocaine. Human services workers served as gatekeepers for these "clients." The gatekeepers were often people who ran programs to help these women. At first the researcher tried to explain to the gatekeepers her interest in the political philosophies of women crack cocaine users who had engaged in sex work. The gatekeepers' perspective on these women emphasized vulnerability rather than political power, and they were not going to allow access to anyone who did not seem to understand the women's weakness. After months of resisting the gatekeepers' characterization of the women she wanted to study, the researcher realized that to gain access, she would have to present herself to the gatekeepers as someone who thought of these women in a very limited way. Luckily, new individuals occupied the gatekeeper position by then, and she was able to break through the barrier they presented by telling them that she would "discuss with the women how difficult and degrading crack cocaine use, prostitution and recovery is for them."[4]

Persistence

Persistence is often required at this stage of access. Sometimes persistence is necessary because the initial contact leads to rejection. For this reason, it is essential to be prepared to revise your approach to the people you want to study. During the process of developing and executing the hook, researchers may find that their preconceived idea(s) about their research get dramatically altered. One reason for this is that when a researcher is testing out his or her hook there are a number of possible responses and reactions. Sometimes the original hook—which worked in a letter or over the phone—does not work as well in face-to-face meetings. Sometimes informants and gatekeepers have their own ideas about what they want the researcher to do, and they may be put off by the researcher's ideas. It may be difficult for the researcher to pinpoint exactly why the hook does not work the way it should. It is even harder to figure out because the same hook may work in some contexts but not in others. Reactions to one's hook can result in closed doors. A closed door, in this context, can also be an opportunity for learning as the researcher clarifies his or her interests or intentions. Researchers who do not have immediate success with their hook are forced to reevaluate it, the research question, and sometimes the research site. As a result, one or all of these may change.

Persistence is also often necessary to obtain multiple points of view. Sometimes multiple initial contacts are required. This is most obvious for researchers learning from individuals who are not in an organizational or institutional context. Such research often requires considerable effort and ingenuity. Our contributors who studied Arab American immigrants, for instance, ran an ad on the radio to increase the number of initial contacts. Interestingly, the radio ad brought in only three responses, but the researchers found that people whom they contacted later had heard the ad and were, perhaps, more ready to talk with them as a result.

Since access to any one site or group of individuals is by no means assured, it may make sense for researchers who want to gain access to multiple sites not to wait until each site or individual makes up its mind but rather to pursue access to multiple sites or individuals simultaneously. This is especially true if one has a limited amount of time in which to conduct one's research—a fellowship or during a research leave, for instance. Several of our contributors experienced long delays in getting approval. Contacting several sites in the same time frame may help ensure that the research is completed within the researcher's time limitations.

Multiple contacts are also important for people whose studies take place in an organizational or institutional context. Even when one has permission to do a study in a particular organization, each person is a new contact, and a new relationship must be established. But researchers also often need to learn from people in multiple organizations. Thus, one contributor made contact with clergy of different churches; another contributor interviewed people from different aspects of the chemical industry. In each of these cases, the interviewees were in an institutional setting that in some ways eased access, but the researcher still had to make repeated initial contacts.

Finally, it is important to follow up. Securing initial access to a site may take several months. During that time period—especially if it is a long one—it is important to keep in contact with the institution that one wishes to study, for it may not tell you as soon as it decides that your proposal has been denied or approved. If the researcher remains in contact and discovers, for example, that the project has been denied, as one of our contributors studying the police did, the researcher can more expeditiously concentrate his or her energies elsewhere.

Persistence is not easy. Researchers who do fieldwork do not self-select on chutzpah. If you happen to be one of those people who do not take it personally when someone says no to you, then you may not need the advice in this section. For many people, however, being denied is a deeply distressing event that makes it difficult to go on and even more difficult to go back to the same place and possibly be denied again. Being rejected multiple times, as in the case of the researcher studying computer companies, can tax a researcher's emotional and material resources. Yet, doing fieldwork often requires this kind of persistence.

Research Implications

There are, of course, questions about whether there is something different about sites and people who agree to share information and those who do not. The answer clearly is yes. But are the differences relevant to the focus of the study?[5] This is a much harder question to answer. Whether one is granted access may simply depend on the receptivity of the individual or group of individuals responsible for granting or denying access, which may vary across and between institutions and individuals. And even if you could somehow gain access to all the research sites you target, would you get all the information you desired? One always wonders about the "one that got away." But as one of our contributors points out, people have the ability to withhold information in a variety of ways. When one gains access, it is partly because people want to share the information they have, and when one is denied access, it is partly because they don't.

Helpful Hints

Here are some of the helpful hints relevant to this stage of the access that are suggested in the stories in part II. Some of these have already been discussed; others have not. We have placed the name of the relevant authors in parentheses for easy reference.

- Gather information when you are waiting for access (Perlow, Sandfort).
- Use downtime to transcribe interviews (Daniel-Echols).
- Use initial contacts to gather information about the organization, the work done, the words used, and so forth (Wrzesniewski, Sandfort).
- Remain in contact with the site while waiting for information about initial entry (Bell).
- Take chances—explore on your own (Garcia-Johnson).
- Customize your letter to contacts when possible (Jelen, Miller-Adams and Myers).
- Think of using other media in order to gain access (e.g., radio) (Jamal and Lin).
- Don't assume that people will respond to you; follow your letter with a call and/or a face-to-face meeting (Jelen).
- Be flexible about sites and about number of sites (Perlow, Bell).
- Dress professionally when talking to professionals (Garcia-Johnson, Miller-Adams and Myers).
- Prioritize your leads in the field (Brooks).
- Learn the language (Sandfort, Miller-Adams and Myers, Garcia-Johnson, Manion).
- Don't appear to know too much (Miller-Adams and Myers).

Notes

1. Richard Nelson Bolles, *What Color Is Your Parachute? A Practical Manual for Job-Hunters and Career-Changers* (Berkeley, Calif.: Ten Speed Press, 1999).

2. A snowball sample is obtained by following the connections provided by several contacts. If each interviewee provides the interviewer with one or two names, the sample quickly grows, much as a snowball does.

3. Martin Hammersley and Paul Atkinson. *Ethnography: Principles in Practice* (New York: Routledge, 1992), 63.

4. See Michele Berger, "Dealing with Difficult Gatekeepers, Vulnerable Populations, and 'Hooks' That Go Awry: An Access Vignette," this volume, pp. 65–68.

5. For interesting discussions of this point, see Colin Brown, Pierre Guillet de Monthoux, and Arthur McCullough, *The Access-Casebook* (Stockholm: Teknisk Högskoletitteratur; Stockholm AB, 1976), and also Brooke Harrington, "The Access Problem: Toward a Theory of Field Research Methods," unpublished manuscript, Brown University, 1999.

Developing Rapport

4

THE NEXT STAGE OF ACCESS involves developing rapport with the people who can provide information. Emphasizing this stage suggests that one can have formal access but not get the needed information. Frequently, it is individuals who hold the key to the information we need. As one researcher has noted, "What good does it do if one is inside yet has no access to information?"[1] Trust is an important part of access and provides a foundation for much of our discussion in this chapter. As Paul Stoller has pointed out, sometimes one simply has to spend time with people in order to know them.[2] Equally important, sometimes one simply has to spend time with people in order for them to know and trust you. This makes sense from a relational perspective as well, since one is more likely to disclose information or communicate with someone one trusts.

Trust

Trust is integral to developing rapport. As Spradley explains, "Rapport refers to a harmonious relationship between ethnographer and informant. It means that a basic sense of trust has developed that allows for the free flow of information."[3] Often the development of trust is reciprocal. The interviewer, through civility, attentive listening, and genuine concern about the informant, comes to be seen as a trustworthy person. Expression of these behaviors is important in any type of research context, but Lin, studying prisons, highlighted how important it was for her in that context (which is often impersonal) to pay extra attention to expressing the aforementioned qualities. She believes this helped facilitate trust and rapport among both staff and inmates.

Trust is particularly important for long-term relationships, in which the researcher engages with informants repeatedly. When researchers have only one contact with the people they are learning from, it is hard to develop trust, and it may not be necessary to do so. People may open up because of their need to express their feelings, much as people are known to share intimate stories with strangers on a train. Of course, even in this instance, informants are unlikely to share information freely if they think there will be negative consequences. In the following, we discuss several aspects of developing rapport and trust.

Commitment Acts

Many of our contributors—particularly those who spent some period of time observing their informants—discuss activities they engaged in that helped to facilitate rapport. Some of these activities involve a particularized investment of time or energy with an unpredictable payoff to the research. Often, there is an element of sacrifice or discomfort in what is being asked of the researcher. Though when undertaken these activities appear unlikely to yield much in the way of a payoff, in the end doing them demonstrates the researcher's commitment to learning the culture of the institution or the people one is studying. We have named these activities "commitment acts."

Commitment acts help foster rapport. Clifford Geertz recounts one of the most famous commitment acts in his discussion of a Balinese cockfight. The article opens with a police raid of a cockfight. Geertz and his wife were in the audience. They followed the lead of the natives and not only ran when the police appeared but also claimed to have no knowledge of the cockfight when the police asked. This was the turning point in their relationship with the people on whom they were dependent for information.

> The next morning the village was a completely different world for us. Not only were we no longer invisible, we were suddenly the center of all attention, the object of a great outpouring of warmth, interest, and most especially, amusement. . . . In Bali, to be teased is to be accepted. It was the turning point so far as our relationship to the community was concerned, and we were quite literally "in."[4]

Commitment acts need not be dramatic to be effective, and we feel it is important to warn researchers against undertaking activities that are dangerous or illegal in order to show their commitment. Quite mundane acts can effectively show your willingness to connect and listen and worthiness to be trusted. For Carol Stack, who was beginning her research on race and poverty, folding newspapers was enough. On her first visit to the neighborhood she wanted to study, she joined a family that was folding newspapers for the oldest son's five evening paper routes. She folded papers for an hour and a half before telling them that she would like to begin a study of family like in this neighborhood. She writes in her book, "Several months later Magnolia told me that she had been surprised that I sat with them that first day to fold papers, and then came back to help again. 'White folks,' she told me 'don't have time, they's always in a rush, and they don't sit on black folk's furniture, at least no Whites that comes into The Flats.'"[5] Of course, Stack engaged in many commitment acts over the next months and years, but this simple gesture early on in the research signaled her willingness to spend time and share space with these people, and it created the opportunity for her to learn from them.

Our contributors demonstrate that many kinds of acts can qualify as commitment acts. One contributor attended an expensive retirement party; another attended a funeral. Others provided expertise or volunteered to help on a project. Some commitment acts were quite mundane but involved enduring the same discomfort that the informants were experiencing. For instance, one contributor talked about continuing her interviews despite the lack of air conditioning on a blistering hot day and on another occasion when the office was filled with the smell of dead rats in the ventilation system.

Although the activities our contributors engaged in were not deliberately undertaken to build rapport, these activities showed a level of engagement that gained the researchers the respect and trust of the people with whom they were building relationships. When a researcher embarks on a commitment act, it is not clear that there will be an explicit gain. That they do not expect to gain by engaging in commitment acts highlights a difference between more traditional information gathering and the building of rapport through commitment acts. While a researcher often assumes information payoff from more traditional research activities, like interviewing or attending meetings, the nature of the commitment acts like those we have described earlier (attending funerals and retirement parties) does not of itself provide a basis for assuming anything is to be gained. Instead, these commitment acts provide an opportunity to create a stronger web of trust, openness, and rapport between researcher and informants. There is no guarantee that any particular act will affect the relationship in a positive way. It may, in fact, be just this quality of commitment acts that makes them work.

Commitment acts also humanize researchers. Through commitment acts, researchers become more than simply people who want information. They step out of their roles and relate to the people in the field site around things that are common to all of us. Births, deaths, retirements, heat, stench, embarrassment, sickness, and other discomforts all provide these opportunities. Even the simple act of sharing food can be a commitment act. Edin's work with the working poor highlights this issue. A woman whom Edin interviewed repeatedly stressed that she had very little to feed her infant except chitlins (pig intestines). Edin "demanded a taste."[6] Suddenly the lack of desirable food choices the woman had was immediately palpable. Edin developed both empathy and rapport with this informant because of this commitment act. Attention to the subtle opportunities frequently involved in rapport building helps researchers become aware of appropriate times to engage in commitment acts.

Identity and Rapport

In the section on initial contact, we described how our participants relied on their professional identities. Identity, personal as well as professional, is even more important to the issue of building rapport. Though we had guessed that particular aspects of researchers' identity, especially their race, gender, class, and professional status, might complicate or make the development of rapport easier, we had not anticipated the vast number of aspects of our identity that seem to matter when attempting to build relationships with individuals. In addition to race, gender, class, and nationality, contributors talked about religion, status as a researcher, place within the organization, and educational background as important parts of their identity that needed to be dealt with in some way while they were obtaining access.

Of course, a person does not have just one identity but rather several: race, class, gender, professional status, nationality, and religion, to name just a few. The intersection of identities can have a powerful effect beyond that of each separate identity.[7] As Sherryl Kleinman, writes, "By bringing a number of identities to interaction, both respondents and researchers get to know each other better and learn to feel comfortable in each other's presence. Also, by broadening the range of relevant identities, researchers can acquire data they might not get otherwise."[8]

We refer to the combined effect of our multiple identities as "intersectionality."[9] In the research process, aspects of our identity often intersect creating a unique experience that is not just race or gender but rather a combination of two or three aspects of identity. Paying attention to intersectionality helps make researchers aware that identities are always dynamic and simultaneously expressed.[10] Among our contributors, we found myriad ways in which their multiple identities interacted in the building of rapport between researcher and informant.

The comments of contributors suggested that identity mattered in ways that they had not expected. This may be in part because as students and scholars, we may believe that when we are engaged in conducting research, "researcher" is the identity that we feel is and should be viewed by others as primary. When doing fieldwork, however, one leaves one's established milieu and identity and goes to another space, where we interact with others who may construct us in various ways. In the following, we discuss how similarities and differences in identity can affect access and also how researchers may try to manipulate the perception of similarity or difference through subtle deception.

How Similarities and Difference Affect Access

Issues of identity at first seem to suggest that the more similar we are to people we are trying to learn from, the more information they may reveal. Some scholars relate social identity theory to the development of trust.[11] From this perspective, similarity can be useful in establishing common ground eventually leading to rapport with informants.[12] One scholar suggests that researchers should assess the interests they have in common with the people they want to research and use that assessment to establish a connection. She suggests that such categories of social identity as demographic characteristics, professional identities, or shared interests can provide the basis for trust. "The researcher's goal is to become identified as a familiar, 'known quantity.' This can involve perceptions of similarity between researchers and the groups they study, or it may require the intercession of boundary-spanning individuals: people whose identities overlap those of the researcher and the group to be studied."[13]

A number of our contributors talked about how similar aspects of identity affected the development of rapport between them and their informants. The most common observation from participants was that their racial identity helped bridge the gap between them as researchers and the individuals they were studying or from whom they needed access. Several participants suggested that sharing a race with one's informants made establishing rapport easier. In these cases, often informal and tacit rules of interaction were experienced and acted on by both researcher and informant.

To the extent that the literature on ethnographic methods engages questions of race, the idea of the "race-matching model" is a central concept.[14] *Racial matching* refers to the intentional focus on racial or ethnic similarities between researcher and informant. The racial matching concept suggests that shared racial or ethnic identity between researcher and informant creates "insider knowledge" for the researcher in relation to the informant and his or her research context. Thus, sharing a racial or ethnic identity can facilitate certain levels of access.[15]

One contributor who studied African American welfare recipients mentioned that the fact that she was herself African American and also a mother (she was visibly pregnant during some of the interviewing) made both the clients and the staff in the welfare-to-work programs she studied feel comfortable with her. The clients sometimes mistook her for one of them and shared freely their feelings about the program. The staff, who were also generally African American, often saw her as someone they wanted to help, as someone who was fulfilling a dream they might have had. They saw their participation as contributing to her education.

Similarity in identity however can, in fact, be double edged. Twine suggests that this focus on "racial insiderness" oversimplifies racial dynamics. She contends that because of the complexity of multiple identities, people of the same ethnic or racial group "do not better [necessarily] understand racism nor do they necessarily identify more closely with members of their racial group."[16] This presumption can lead the informant to assume a commonality of experience that might increase trust but decrease the need for explanations. As a result, informants who assume similarity in identity may gloss over information that the researcher might want to have or need to have spelled out. This is one of the disadvantages of becoming a participant in the research site. In this kind of research, the researcher's identity does change and become similar to the identity of the people in the field site. When this happens, it is hard to ask the naïve questions that an outsider can ask and hard for informants to answer these questions fully.

Similarity may ease some aspects of access but does not always increase information. Sometimes people tell more because they assume that the researcher does not understand their perspective. Just as some contributors found that their difference in ethnicity was useful for drawing out explanations, other contributors felt that differences in race and gender, or gender and nationality, had a positive effect on developing rapport or gaining information. One contributor, an African American woman who studied a police department hate crime unit found that sometimes the combined effect of race and gender could be useful in drawing out explanations and establishing rapport with detectives who were white and male. She found that detectives who were white and male took pains to explain not only concepts that they felt a layperson might need to know but also their own perspectives, which they may have felt she, as someone who was "different," might not have been able to appreciate. This process led to fuller explanations. With these longer, more personal vignettes came the development of rapport between the detectives and the contributor.

Another contributor, a Mexican American woman who traveled to Brazil and Mexico to interview NGO activists and business elites about environmental issues in the chemical industry, felt that being young and different in gender and nationality helped her older male informants let down their guard with her. She also found that industrialists in the chemical industry were eager to speak with her because they wanted to show her that they cared about the environment too.

Difference in identity can likewise be an obstacle to access. This can be especially true for those studying abroad. For women studying in cultures in which women performs roles very different from those in the United States, gender can shape access.[17] One contributor who studied in Bosnia felt that the combination of her gender, nationality, and marital status impeded access to male informants. Because she was a young, single American woman, it was less appropriate for her to be talking with men. She found she generally gained more information from women than from men. Another contributor, a young Canadian woman who interviewed Chinese cadres, had a difficult time setting up a space to interview young men where the interview could not be overheard. Here differences in both gender and nationality play a role. Had she been a Chinese woman, it might still have been considered inappropriate for her to be alone with the men, but there would not have been the possibility of an international scandal. Though her gender served as a barrier to access to younger men, another aspect of her identity—age—removed obstacles in setting up interviews with older Chinese men. The combined—or intersectional—effect of different aspects of these researchers' identities contributed to their gaining access and developing rapport with some individuals but not others.

Collaborative work further complicates the discussion of how similarities and differences affect access. As both Bhavnani and Davis note, joint research relationships "rarely unfold without complications."[18] One of the projects described in part II makes use of both similarity and difference in identity. The research project involved interviewing Arab American immigrants about their political socialization and activity. One of the researchers was a member of the Arab American community; the other researcher was Chinese American. The two used the combination of their ethnic similarity and difference to help them gather information. For a joint research project, the similarity of the Arab American researcher to their interviewees allowed them to conduct the interviews in Arabic when it would have been difficult or embarrassing to explain things in English. At the same time, the difference of having an Asian American researcher present gave them an opportunity to ask for explanations when such a request would be annoying coming from a knowledgeable cultural insider.

Deception and Rapport

Researchers may at times engage in deception, because they think it will increase their rapport with informants and therefore their access to information. "The decision to deceive generally rests on a concern to ensure the most natural behavior among research participants."[19] One form of deception that appears to be quite commonly practiced is to conceal aspects of one's "true identity."[20] Such deception may be most pronounced for researchers doing fieldwork involving extended interactions with their informants. For these researchers, the development of trust is particularly important, and there are many opportunities for researchers and informants to get to know one another.

While we have no contributors who concealed the fact that they were doing research, a number of our contributors report engaging in deceptions of various sorts. For the most part, the efforts were intended to make the researchers seem more like the people they were interviewing. Contributors, for instance, report suppressing differences of opinion they have with their informants or highlighting similarities. People, for example, also concealed or obscured their class in several instances. One contributor concealed her undergraduate institution, a highly prestigious private school. Another allowed the people she was interviewing to assume that she, like them, would never own an expensive house in an upper-middle-class suburb, something that she already had. Another contributor wore one set of clothes to go to the interview and another for the interview itself. She was interviewing business leaders in poverty-stricken countries but was living on a tight budget and staying in poorer sections of town, and she felt it might be dangerous to leave her hotel in her professional clothes. At the same time, she felt it important to wear professional clothes if the interviews were to be taken seriously.

These deceptions were significant enough that our contributors remembered them. This is, in part, because of the unusual nature of the relationship that the researcher enters into. The relationship is highly asymmetrical. Unlike in a friendship, there is no attempt for both persons to know equal amounts about the other. Researchers seek to know a great deal about the informants and try to reveal as little as possible about themselves. As others have recognized, these deceptions are not unlike the small deceptions practiced in many relationships, though there may be more conscious and more consistent impression management for the field worker. "One cannot bias the fieldwork by talking only with people one finds most congenial or politically sympathetic: one cannot choose one's informants on the same basis as one chooses one's friends."[21]

Our contributors report mixed success with deception. A number of them report concern about exposure, the threat of which was anxiety provoking. For instance, one of our contributors who studied an American automobile company drove a car made by a Japanese automobile company. Though he had not identified himself as a driver of any particular kind of car, when an informant tried to take him back to his car after a lunch meeting, he felt the threat of exposure. Though he avoided it, the fear is palpable in his vignette.

It is never clear how much these deceptions matter. One scholar argues that there is often more room for "directness and honesty" than researchers might believe and suggests that honesty may make the research better.[22] Only two of our contributors report what they felt to be serious exposures of their deceptions. In one case, the exposure did not occur around the informants but on her way to an interview. She simply got off the bus and took another bus to her interview. In the other instance, a contributor who had tried to conceal her class background forgot and wore her Ivy League ring to the field site one day. It was noticed immediately, but there is no evidence that the exposure had any effect on the research.

Not only is it unclear how much exposure of these deceptions matter, but it is also unclear how much control one ever has over how informants will see you.

One scholar writes about trying to be very open and telling everyone about his background and his current role in a particular study, only to find that the people he was learning from had made up stories about him over which he had no control.[23] Many of our contributors found themselves classified in ways that made their informants comfortable but took some adjustment for the researcher. Informants can increase or decrease one's status or change it altogether. They may, for instance, innocently demote you to intern or promote you to professor. Some contributors feared that correcting informants by reminding them of their "true identity" might damage rapport. Other contributors found that their repeated efforts to remind their informants of their "true" identities made no difference.

Rapport, Identity, and Flexibility

Some research involved contributors taking on substantially different identities. This involved them showing flexibility in thinking about who they were. Almost by definition, this occurs for people who become true participant observers. One of our contributors became an Amway distributor and undertook a lifestyle quite different from before and after the study. Two others went to work for bureaucracies. Their identities during this time were quite unlike their identities as students and researchers. As we know from examples of people who leave academia after doing such research (Rosen comes immediately to mind), such flexibility is anything but superficial.[24] As indicated in several vignettes, confusion and emotional distress are not unusual when the researcher engages in this kind of flexibility.

Dealing with Identity

Thinking about identity is clearly important for assessing likely access to information. There are few regularities, however. Sometimes situations arise in which one's identity clearly eases or creates challenges for access. Often, however, one finds that identity issues cut both ways or that the same identity cuts different ways for different people. Rather than propose some hard and fast rule about the effect of identity, we think the importance of thinking about identity is awareness. It is useful in assessing the information that you receive to be aware of how one's identity may influence why some people are providing information and others are withholding it.

Identity is important not only in relation to the people one is studying but also in relation to oneself. Our own identities or subjectivities enable us to understand some information better than other information. One of our contributors, Ernestine Enomoto, for instance, found that her former experience as a math teacher influenced both the individuals with whom she interacted with during her fieldwork in an inner-city high school and how she understood what they were saying. She felt it was important to recognize this potential bias rather than to assume it away because it was not scientific. She drew on Peshkin to make this point. He writes, "[B]y monitoring myself, I can create an illuminating, empowering personal statement that attunes me to where self and subject are intertwined. I do not, thereby exorcise my subjectivity. I do, rather, enable myself to manage it—to preclude its becoming unwittingly burdensome—as I progress through collecting, analyzing and writing up my data."[25]

Helpful Hints

Here are some of the helpful hints relevant to this stage of the access that are suggested in the stories in part II. Some of these have been discussed earlier; others have not. We have placed the name of the relevant authors in parentheses for easy reference.

- Show your commitment (Daniel-Echols).
- Use the aspects of your identity that are most relevant to your audience. These may not be the most relevant to you or to some other audience (Schermer, Perlow, Feldman).
- If conducting joint research, utilize perceived differences and similarities of researchers (Jamal and Lin).
- Be aware of how you might have to balance identities that come into conflict (e.g., employee and observer) (Pratt, Ginger).
- Sometimes it is a good idea to blend in (Garcia-Johnson).
- Be aware of your subjectivities (Enomoto).

Notes

1. Barbara Czarniawska, *A Narrative Approach to Organization Studies* (Thousand Oaks, Calif.: Sage, 1998), 39.

2. Paul Stoller, *The Taste of Ethnographic Things: The Senses in Anthropology* (Philadelphia: University of Pennsylvania Press, 1989), especially chap. 8.

3. Spradley, *The Ethnographic Interview*, 78.

4. Clifford Geertz, "Deep Play: Notes on the Balinese Cockfight," in *Interpretive Social Science: A Reader*, ed. Paul Rabinow and William Sullivan (Berkeley: University of California Press, 1979), 185.

5. Carol B. Stack, *All Our Kin: Strategies for Survival in a Black Community* (New York: Harper & Row, 1974).

6. Jason DeParle, "Learning Poverty Firsthand," *New York Times*, 27 April 1997, 32.

7. See Kimberle Williams Crenshaw, "Demarginalizing the Intersection of Race and Sex: A Black Feminist Critique of Anti-Discrimination Doctrine, Feminist Theory, and Antiracist Politics," in *Feminist Legal Theory: Readings in Law and Gender*, ed. Katherine T. Bartlett and Roseanne Kennedy (New York: Westview, 1991).

8. See Sherryl Kleinman, "Learning the Ropes as Fieldwork Analysis," in *Fieldwork Experience: Qualitative Approaches to Social Research*, ed. William Shaffier, Robert A. Stebbins, and Allan Turowetz (New York: St. Martin's, 1980), 181.

9. Michele Berger, "Workable Sisterhood: A Study of the Political Participation of Stigmatized Women with HIV/AIDS," Ph.D. diss., University of Michigan, 1998.

10. See France Winddance Twine and Jonathan Warren, eds., *Racing Research/Researching Race: Methodological Dilemmas in Critical Race Studies* (New York: New York University Press, 2000). On multiple identities, see Philomena Essed, *Understanding Everyday Racism: An Interdisciplinary Theory* (Newbury Park, Calif.: Sage, 1991).

11. Brooke Harrington, "The Access Problem: Toward a Theory of Field Research Methods," unpublished manuscript, Brown University, 1999; Kleinman, "Learning the Ropes"; Joan E. Hoffman, "Problems of Access in the Study of Social Elites and Boards of Directors," in *Fieldwork Experience: Qualitative Approaches to Social Research*, ed. William Shaffier, Robert A. Stebbins, and Allan Turowetz (New York: St. Martin's, 1980), 51; Takeyuki Tsuda, "Ethnicity and the Anthropologist: Negotiating Identities in the Field," *Anthropological Quarterly* 71, no. 3 (July 1998): 878–90.

12. See, for example, Kleinman, "Learning the Ropes," 179–80.

13. Harrington, "The Access Problem," 25.

14. See Frances Winddance Twine, "Racial Ideologies and Racial Methodologies," in *Racing Research/Researching Race*, ed. Frances Winddance Twine and Jonathan Warren, 1–34.

15. Twine and Warren, *Racing Research/Researching Race.*

16. Twine and Warren, *Racing Research/Researching Race.*

17. See Loes Schenk-Sandbergen, "Gender in Field Research: Experiences in India," in *Anthropological Journeys: Reflections on Fieldwork*, ed. Meenakshi Thapan (New Delhi: Orient Longman, 1998), 267–89.

18. Bhavnani and Davis, *Women in Prison,* 227–45.

19. Corrine Glesne and Alan Peshkin, *Becoming Qualitative Researchers* (White Plains, N.Y.: Longman, 1992), 120.

20. Martin Hammersley and Paul Atkinson, *Ethnography: Principles in Practice* (New York: Routledge, 1992), 68–72.

21. Hammersley and Atkinson, *Ethnography,* 84.

22. Michael Agar, *The Professional Stranger: An Informal Introduction to Ethnography* (Orlando, Fla.: Academic Press), 60. Sieber makes similar point in *Planning Ethically Responsible Research.*

23. Agar, *The Professional Stranger,* 60.

24. Michael Rosen, *Turning Words, Spinning Worlds* (Singapore: Harwood Academic Publishers, 2000).

25. Peshkin, *The Color of Strangers, the Color of Friends: The Play of Ethnicity in School and Community* (Chicago: University of Chicago Press, 1991), 294.

Exiting: Ending the Relationship 5

THOUGH THIS BOOK IS ABOUT "GETTING IN" to research sites and gaining access to information from individuals, we would be remiss if we did not at least address the important issue of leaving, or getting out. Exit is the final stage of access. Thus, it signals the end of one stage of the research process. Feelings of loss after exit underscore the importance of seeing access as a relationship involving a series of processes—doing preparatory work, making a proposal, getting it accepted, and developing rapport with individuals—rather than a single unitary transaction of getting in. The relational perspective suggests that exit is a part of access. Exit is the end of, or at least a change in, the relationship that provides access. This relational perspective helps explain the grief researchers often feel upon exit and the regret they often experience about how they exit.

In some ways, the relational analogy is an awkward fit with respect to the process of exit. We do not often enter into relationships/friendships with the understanding that we need to think about how to end them. Consciousness that the relationship will end, or at least change, however, does not prevent researchers from forming relationships that are very genuine and that are difficult and, sometimes, painful, to end. Academia provides any number of analogies. Graduate students form close relationships with faculty and other students, knowing that once they finish their degrees, their relationships will change and that some of them will end. People develop relationships while they are on postdoctoral fellowships that they know will change at the end of the fellowships. While one enters into these situations with the knowledge that the relationships formed will change, one enters into them nonetheless. Time provides a boundary for research projects in much the same way that it provides a boundary for these other relationships.

Just as other temporally bound relationships sometimes survive changes in location or focus, relationships formed through research do not always end. The type of research is one factor that influences the likelihood that relationships formed will continue after the research has ended. Research involving extended observation or membership, as discussed in chapters 9 and 10, tends to create bonds that are harder to break than research that does not involve as much shared time with the informants.

A number of contributors expressed regret about their exits from research sites. Several worried that they had not "thanked" their informants adequately. We referred earlier to the fact that several researchers found individuals in their research sites willing to help in ways that primarily benefited the researchers and seemed of little benefit to the informants. This left several researchers searching for something they could do for the people that had helped them and worried that they had not done enough to repay their informants' generosity. The informants in one study of cleaners at a local university hospital showed powerful emotions and shared personal vignettes and painful experiences in their interviews. In such instances, the researchers noted that it felt awkward to offer only a coffee cup and a promise of the transcript and a research report. Like others who establish strong connections with their informants, these contributors felt they had not done enough to give back to their subjects. The more emotion their subjects displayed, the more the researchers may have felt pulled to "do something."[1]

Leaving the Field

We asked our contributors to discuss how they exited or left the site and whether they had exited in ways that allowed them to regain or maintain access to the sites. The experiences of our contributors suggest that those who leave the field do so mainly for two reasons. The first is expected: Researchers stop gathering data when they have collected a sufficient amount of data, or they feel that they are not learning anything "new."

Surprisingly, having collected large amounts of data did not by itself signal to all contributors that they should leave the research site. The second reason people left the field is that life events intervened, creating circumstances that made collecting data much more inconvenient. One contributor, for instance, was on the edge of ending data collection when he awoke one morning to a snowstorm, contemplated the commute from home to his field site, and decided that his fieldwork was over. This vignette highlights how life events can make the incremental gain posed by one more day or one more week in the field appear very small.

Irrespective of what eventually determines exit, the contributions in this volume suggest that leaving the field is significant enough that those in the process of designing research should think about their exit before they begin the research. This is true for several reasons. First, and perhaps most important, for some, leaving the research site forecloses further information gathering. Many, once they leave, cannot go back and gather information in the same way. For some who study in other countries or even in another city, the cost of return to the site is very high. Even if the research site is geographically accessible, leaving the field often breaks the dynamic of trust and communication that the frequent contact of being in the field can create.

Exiting in Stages

It was hard for contributors to exit abruptly. In part, they worried about having collected enough data or about having additional questions. Several contributors indicated they planned the research in a way that allowed them to come back to the research site at later points and gather additional data. In this way, researchers were able to exit in stages, gradually.

For many, keeping open the option of returning to the site at a later date entailed alerting those in the site ahead of time that permission for return visits was needed, providing those in the site with preliminary findings, and keeping in contact with individuals in the site during the separation. Several of our contributors returned to the research sites for brief visits before concluding in-person data collection. One such contributor who studied welfare offices made periodic phone calls to key informants to ask them questions and learn about developments that had transpired since she had left. Having remained in contact with them, reentry was much easier when she needed to return to her sites.

Continuing Engagement

Not all of our contributors had the option of exiting the field. For personal reasons, some of our contributors had to conduct their research in ways that reflected the fact that they were going to maintain connections with their research subjects. Two contributors studying the Arab American community noted that exit was not an option, since the Arab American researcher in the pair had been involved with the community before the project and would remain a part of it after the project was over. Another contributor was not a part of the community she was studying; instead, she formed a number of close relationships with her informants that would have been difficult to end abruptly. She elected to ease her own emotional stress by not abruptly disengaging from her informants but, rather, maintaining relationships with e-mails, notes, and letters.

Thinking about Exit

Whether one exits abruptly, gradually, in stages, or does not have the option of exit, our contributors' access vignettes reveal that the issue of how one leaves the site is important. Planning and preparation is required if one wants to regain entry to the site. Planning how to exit and how to thank one's informants may help reduce misgivings at this stage of the research.

The regret and emotional trauma that some of our contributors experienced upon leaving the field suggest that researchers would do well to think long and hard about exit, not only before they begin but also while they conduct the research, so that they can exit "well."

Helpful Hints

Listed here are some of the helpful hints relevant to this stage of the access that are suggested in the stories in part II. Some of these have been discussed already; others have not. We have placed the names of the relevant authors in parentheses for easy reference.

- Take time to think about how you will exit, and thank informants (Wrzesniewski, Dutton and Debebe).
- Ask to be kept on mailing lists (Ginger).
- Take time to send articles and other materials that arise from your work (Ginger).
- If you think you may want to reenter the field, prepare informants for your initial exit and then give estimates of when you might return. Discuss whether you will ask the same types of things from them when you reenter the research site (i.e., conducting interviews, looking at files, etc.) (Daniel-Echols).
- Be prepared to experience varied feelings and in some cases conflicted loyalties (Pratt).

Note

1. For a short discussion of this point, see Ester Heffernan, *Making It in Prison: The Square, the Cool, and the Life* (New York: Wiley, 1972).

GAINING ACCESS: THE INSIDE STORIES

II

Gaining Access to Individuals 6

LL OF THE ACCESS STORIES in this volume describe the experience of researchers who have gained access to individuals. Although institutions mediate access in various ways, we take the relationship between individual researcher and individual informant as the fundamental base of the access relationship. Therefore, even though many of the access stories we present involve individuals that belong to either a common organizational context or a network of organizations, we begin with four stories that do not. These stories portray a range of levels of access, from single interviews to multiple interviews and observation.

Though the researchers in this chapter desired different levels of access, there is an important issue linking all researchers who seek access to unaffiliated individuals—the challenge of finding informants. To obtain access to individuals who are not part of an organization one must develop trust with them one by one. The researcher cannot rely on a common structure either to identify appropriate informants or to vouch for the researcher's trustworthiness. In this chapter we describe the challenges of finding informants and developing trust with them.

Preparation

Depending on the level of access required by the researcher, gaining access to individuals may require years of preparation. Researchers often need to develop reputations for consistency and integrity in ways that are seemingly peripheral to their research and quite diffuse. This may require that researchers live in the community and display their commitment to the community before they will be trusted with the information they seek. Ann Cornelisen in *Women of the Shadows*[1] and Paul Stoller in *The Taste of Ethnographic Things*[2] both emphasize the difference that such a reputation can make as they relate how multiple informants consistently misrepresent aspects of their lives to researchers who have not established such reputations. In all of the stories we present here, such reputations were important. In three of the stories, the researchers lived or had lived in the community and had extensive networks of friends and associates who could vouch for them.

Researchers often need to learn new languages to relate to their informants. This is most obvious in the case of researchers who do their work in countries other than their own, but it is also true of other researchers. Spradley notes that the learning of a new language is part of what makes the difference between an informant and a respondent.[3] He points out that informants are "native speakers" who help the researcher learn the language or dialect and provide models for researchers to imitate. This is equally important if the researcher's field site is halfway around the world or if it is in an office across the street. Learning what people mean when they use particular words or phrases in particular contexts is important not only for understanding what they are telling the researcher but also, at a deeper level, for enhancing trust in the relationship between researchers and informant, thereby increasing the information that the informant is comfortable sharing.

Finding Informants

Once the researcher has prepared him- or herself, finding the right individuals to interview or observe can be a major challenge, especially if one is studying individuals not connected to an organization. William Foote Whyte relates one of the most famous stories of finding an informant in the appendix to *Street Corner Society*.[4] He recounts trying several different approaches before he entered through the "door" of a settlement house where a social worker introduced him to "Doc." Once he found Doc, he entered into a world that would have been, at best, opaque to him without Doc. Whyte does not tell how long it took for him to connect with Doc, but weeks or even months seem likely.

Often very early in the access process it becomes important for a researcher to have someone of the community to vouch for his or her presence. This is conveyed in a famous study of lower-income African American men in Elliot Liebow's *Tally's Corner*.[5] Although "Tally" was a primary respondent, Liebow had to negotiate many potential respondents that hung out at the Carry Out, a neighborhood grocery. Even though he was beginning to build trust with Tally, Liebow was warned that he would need to be concerned with others who were suspicious of him and his motives. Within the first few weeks of his fieldwork, he was however, able to have someone vouch for his identity:

> At the Downtown café the man who told me that I'd be okay if I knew "one or two of the right people" publicly identified me as his friend. ("Sure I know him,"

he told another man in my presence. "We had a long talk the other day. He's my friend and he's okay, man he's okay. At first I thought he was a cop, but he's no cop. He's okay.")[6]

Having someone who can introduce you to people and possibly protect you during the process of finding respondents can become very important. Additionally, having someone who will vouch for you in the field can help the researcher build webs of relationships. Being identified early on with certain people can aid a researcher and provide both lateral and vertical connections to people. Eckstein, who was studying the conditions of the Mexican poor, encountered a prestige hierarchy during the process of access. She relates:

> Once seen in the presence of local elites I generally had no difficulty establishing rapport with their subordinates, either because the elites told their subordinates to collaborate with me or because the lower-ranking functionaries assumed they could and should follow the example of their hierarchal superior and talk with me if I approached them. The prestige hierarchy in the community, in sum, had a "halo" effect, which readily facilitated my research.[7]

Often the researcher does not know exactly which individual can facilitate access to other informants. Reflecting on this point, one researcher studying female artists in St. Louis remarked that her informants were not a group and did not have a site; thus, it became part of her research to identify them. "I could not simply go somewhere, watch what happened there, and ask questions about it; first I had to find people and determine the shape and locales of their world."[8] The task of finding unaffiliated informants frequently requires assessing continuously the range of people encountered in the field and taking advantage of any opportunity that presents itself. Studs Terkel, who based his book *Working* on interviews with workers from many different walks of life, was challenged by the task of getting access to multiple informants. Improvisation and chance, Terkel reveals in the introduction to his book, played a role in finding informants. He writes:

> While riding the el, I was approached by a singularly tall stranger. Hearing me talking (as I have a habit of doing), he recognized my voice as "the man he listens to on the radio." He told me of his work and his father's work's. . . . He told me of two of his students: a young hospital aide and a young black man who works in a bank. They, too, are in this book.[9]

Many researchers like Terkel have sought and gained access to individuals who are not connected by a common organizational context.[10] In the book *The Ethnographic Interview*, James Spradley relates his understanding of access based on numerous projects of his own as well as the supervision of many students.[11] He describes the development of informants as a relational process that is highly dependent on features that the researcher may have little control over. These include the match of personalities between researcher and informant, cultural norms of the informant, and the interpersonal skills of the researcher.

Identity can be an important link between researcher and informant. Edin's research with the working poor provides a useful example of the resourcefulness needed to find common ground with multiple individuals.[12] Edin, a white woman, skillfully used her identity as a mother and also as a parent of African American and multiethnic children to connect with many lower-income families.

Gatekeepers

Researchers may also need to establish a relationship with gatekeepers to gain access to multiple informants. These gatekeepers may be individuals but are often organizations. In this sense, organizations are important even when the researcher is not at all interested in the organizational connection. Whyte, for instance, gained access through a settlement house. Spradley gained access for one of his studies through a local jail. As discussed in chapter 3, encountering gatekeepers can be a problem. While they have contacts to large numbers of individual people, they may also prevent access that the informants would allow. To gain access to HIV-positive sex workers, one of our contributors, Berger, was forced to change how she talked about her research to conform to gatekeepers' attitudes about the women's behavior. She was granted access to the population she wished to study only when she talked about the women being studied in a way that was in line with the gatekeepers' hidden agendas, ideologies, and cultures.

Trust between a Researcher and Informant

Both Spradley and Whyte emphasize creating and maintaining trust between researcher and informant in their accounts of gaining access. Trust is context dependent. This is particularly evident when the informants are not connected by a common organizational context where the researcher's reputation, if positive, can ease the connection from one person to the next. Some of the researchers whose stories are included in this section needed to connect with multiple informants but did not need to have extended connections. Instead, they needed to develop trust repeatedly with different informants, only some of whom would have had contact with other informants. Multiple informants may appear to make any particular informant less important, but each person's viewpoint is critical to the understanding the researcher gains. Convincing people to reveal their worlds is hardly ever easy.

Trust is also a major component of obtaining access when, as in the stories reported in this section, researchers are asking their respondents to talk about issues that are politically and personally sensitive. Building trust requires establishing strong, respectful ties with respondents. For Edin, building trust with informants often meant overlooking situations and conditions that might have made other researchers uncomfortable (e.g., conducting an interview in a housing project with an armed gang member outside the door). Moreover, Edin not only continued her research despite these situations but, when possible, set up play dates between her kids and some of the informants' kids. Fenno reminds us that trust is "less a special talent than a special willingness to work hard—a special commitment. And one reason it is hard work is because of the many contexts and types of people you find yourself confronted with."[13]

If one is studying marginalized, hidden, or heavily stigmatized individuals, the challenges in gaining access and developing trust are magnified. Individuals in these populations may prove both harder to identify and harder to find because of their membership in stigmatized groups. Some individuals marginalized from groups may be suspicious of the researchers' aims and may be hesitant to allow access. All of the access stories that follow involve sensitive issues, and three involve populations that are relatively marginalized. Manion talks with Chinese cadres about the establishment norm in a system that has never had one. Both the Bosnian ethnic minorities that Pickering studied and the Arab immigrants in the United States that Jamal and Lin studied could pay a heavy price for opening up to the wrong people. The HIV-positive sex workers that Berger studied appear to have nothing to lose, but they are so heavily stigmatized that they have a hard time believing that Berger wants to learn from them rather than further stigmatize them. These researchers report the difficulty of, and their strategies for, convincing people to open up in this context. The strategies vary by the context, but an overall theme prevails: Show sincere respect for these people and for what you can learn from them, and some of them will come to trust you and confide in you. This is clearly not a responsibility to be taken lightly.

Maintaining Access

Amaney Jamal and Ann Chih Lin

Gaining access is generally understood as coming "first" in a research project. But as the following anecdote explains, access is a continual task whose success is always uncertain. A year into our project on Arab immigrant political socialization and activity, we decided to try to recruit respondents through radio ads. We wrote a one-minute message that was broadcast three times daily on the local Arabic radio stations, and then we sat back and waited for the calls to start rolling in. Two weeks later, we had a grand total of three responses.

But the story does not end here. Although few people called us in direct response to our advertisement, we found people mentioning the ad when we went up to them on the street. "I heard about you on the radio," an immigrant would say in response to Jamal's opening approach. "Sure, I will be glad to help." Clearly, hearing about us on the radio made people more receptive to listening to our description of the project and our request for an interview. It gave us credibility as well as visibility.

This incident illustrates a number of issues we encountered as we sought to gain and maintain access to a diffuse "community"—the population of first-generation Arab immigrants living in the Detroit metropolitan area. Unlike researchers in organizations, we did not have a gatekeeper to go to for access. Instead, to *gain* and *maintain* access, we repeated the process of getting access every time we approached a new person for an interview.[14]

Gaining Access: Does Insider Status Facilitate the Research Agenda?

We had the incomparable advantage of being known to many in the community as we started. Jamal, an Arab American, is well known in Arab American circles in the Detroit area, and she is a fluent Arabic speaker who wears the *hijab*, or Muslim head scarf. At the same time, the professional credibility we established, both through our institutional affiliation with the University of Michigan and through our various assurances of confidentiality, was crucial. But without question, the most important thing we did was simply to ask, explain, and ask again, with the understanding that we were in the community to stay.

When we began this project, we knew our biggest asset was Jamal's insider status. We were deeply concerned that our respondents might be afraid that we were affiliated with a government agency—especially the FBI or INS, both of which are believed to target immigrants. Lin's outsider status exacerbated these concerns: If not for some nefarious purpose, why would an outsider want to know so much? Jamal's appearance and language, however, immediately identified her as a member of the community. Her connections and referrals provided a set of networks to get us started, and her presence was critical in convincing people to listen to us and in vouching for Lin, a Chinese American.

The dynamic changed somewhat once we began to interview. We found there were advantages to pairing an outsider with an insider: Respondents exerted themselves to explain things to Lin that they thought she would not otherwise understand. This allowed us to get a better perspective on their reasoning. Lin's outsider status also allowed her to ask basic questions, questions that would have seemed laughable from an insider. At the same time, Jamal's insider role meant that respondents felt comfortable moving into Arabic when they wished to elaborate on a point or explaining something that they might be shy about saying in front of an outsider.

Despite this pairing, however, the burdens of access clearly fell most heavily on Jamal. She struggled with the vulnerability of blending her professional identity as a student of political science with her personal identity as a well-known parent, friend, and community member. She had to be responsible for Lin's actions as well as her own. She knew that anything that might offend the community or compromise her research objectives could ultimately lead to a two-edged condemnation: one professional, the other personal.

Nor was Jamal's insider status enough, on its own, to guarantee us access. Given the close-knit networks that exist in the area, people were reluctant to speak to anyone they did not know personally or trust. Our project seeks to understand how experiences in one's country of origin and in the United States help socialize individuals into an understanding of U.S. politics and into a U.S. ethnic community. We asked about activities in the United States; acquaintances, families of origin, spouses and children; political experience and affiliations; and religious and social beliefs. This kind of information is hard for anyone to discuss, but within an immigrant population it is especially sensitive. Here Jamal's insider status, crucial in establishing contacts, could have also created hurdles for us. Would interviewees be less willing to talk about their lives to someone who might know them or whom they might see again at community functions or events? So although Jamal's presence was pertinent in getting our "foot in the door," it alone did not ensure cooperation, or the *maintenance* of access. The only way we could reduce (though never eliminate) the anxiety or speculation was to explain adequately our professional roles and obligations. The key to establishing this was our professional credentials, represented first and foremost by our various assurances of confidentiality and anonymity.

Maintaining Confidentiality, Maintaining Access

Confidentiality is at the heart of most research designs involving research with people. In this process, the University of Michigan's institutional review board was an ally. We made copies of our human subjects approval and explained it to our respondents, so that they could see that we were constrained by our academic institution and its guidelines. With IRB support, we did not use written consent, knowing that respondents might want to avoid having their names in a file. Instead, we asked the interim dean of the University of Michigan School of Public

Policy, where Lin teaches, to write a letter explaining our project, our roles, and our respondents' right to withdraw their participation at any time.

By providing these documents and explaining our project at the beginning of the interviews, we ultimately reduced the speculation and anxiety about the nature of our work. We anticipated our respondents' fears of being identified and used familiar language to explain how we safeguarded their identities. We gave respondents the choice of being taped. We further explained that they could quit or ask to skip a question at any time.

These procedures are the norm in many research circles. But for us they were not a mere professional responsibility: They were a central aspect of our self-presentation. Our care in explaining and emphasizing confidentiality, both in our initial contacts and again at the time of the interview, was critical to our ability to *maintain* access. The dense nature of community ties meant that our reputation would precede us: One successful interview could lead to others, and one unsuccessful interview could ruin the environment of "good faith" we had diligently worked to create. If we had made individuals feel at any point that we were not being "professionally" considerate of their disclosures, we would have closed multiple doors.

Asking and Staying

The need to be both persuasive and trustworthy requires one to think about the presentation of self. For Jamal, commonly accepted procedures, like reading a script to potential interviewees at the time of contact, seemed unnatural. She was concerned about the success of the overall project and whether she could find a balance between both her Arabness and professionalism. Could she present herself as an objective observer in her own community? Would her natural empathy imply that she was not being a professional researcher? Would others expect her to be an advocate, activist, or lobbyist rather than an academic researcher? And if so, how could she maintain her professional role without creating barriers between herself and the community?

She dealt with these concerns by telling potential respondents about her motivation for starting the project: her sense that Arab Americans had been greatly misrepresented as an ethnic group. In her introductions, she made it clear that she was a student of political science and that she wanted to learn more about Arab Americans as an immigrant community. Taking sufficient time to discuss not only the project but her own studies as a doctoral student helped Jamal work through her own as well as our respondents' concerns.

The response was overwhelmingly positive. Our turn-down rate was very low in cases where sufficient phone conversations and discussions took place prior to asking for an interview. When adequate conversation did not take place, we were less successful. So we continued to take the time to talk to people. When we decided to increase our number of access points in the community by approaching social service organizations, going into stores, or talking to people on the street in Arab neighborhoods, we were careful to be generous with our time and sincere in our interactions. This could translate into hours on end helping store owners and drinking tea while awaiting potential interviewees.

The problem in not establishing sufficient rapport is that researchers can easily be classified as exploiters of a community's information, not people committed to the welfare of the community itself. When doing research in an organization, expectations about the dissemination and use of the results are often part of a research agreement worked out with the organization. By contrast, when working with a diffuse population, the question of responsibility is less explicit but no less present. The complications are compounded when doing research in one's own community. For Jamal, "exit" is not an option; she was involved with the community before the project and will continue to be a part of the community afterward.

For us, currently in the middle of the research, what this means in terms of our ongoing relationship with the community is still under construction. But it underlines the ways in which gaining access and maintaining access are two dependent and reciprocal processes of one's research. To gain access is not only to obtain initial approval but also to maintain the integrity of the privilege granted to the researcher. This maintenance is what allows for greater access.

Chinese Officials as Ordinary Respondents

Melanie Manion

In mid-1986, I set out for China as a graduate student to research an unusually difficult example of the party-state effort to build social norms from public policies: the replacement of de facto lifelong tenure for officials with regular age-based retirement. The policy, introduced in 1978, had little precedent. It broke with the tradition of political purge that stigmatizes exit from office under communism. It challenged the vested interests of 2.5 million veteran revolutionaries, who had monopolized power in party and government for most of the years since communist victory in 1949. It contradicted the basis of their hold on power, revolutionary seniority, as well as still prevalent traditional Chinese views about age and authority.[15]

Formulated as a question about norm building, my research required that I interview already retired officials and also younger officials, whom I expected to be the policy's most eager informal enforcers. These sorts of interviews constituted a new challenge in the study of Chinese politics: Party and government officials were to be neither interpreters of official policy, interviewed in the politically monitored environment of a government office in Beijing, nor informants about the workings of the system, interviewed in the more politically relaxed environment of Hong Kong. Rather, older and younger officials were *ordinary respondents,* candidly representing no more and no less than their own personal experiences and opinions. Meeting the challenge of finding these officials, establishing rapport, and interviewing them as ordinary respondents in the mainland Chinese context of the mid-1980s constitute the focus of my access story.

Finding Respondents

To find officials who would talk about themselves frankly and freely, I needed the intervention of friends willing to present me to these officials as someone worthy of their confidences. In the case of older officials, whose advanced age, long association with the regime, and, in some cases, high rank did not incline them to trust a young foreign student, this sort of intervention was all the more important.

It takes time to make friends anywhere, but more so in a foreign culture and language, time that is not part of the normal dissertation research schedule for which grants are provided. I chose Peking University as my institutional affiliation, because I had friends there from my student years in the late 1970s, a time when foreigners in China were scarcer and more closely monitored. For administrators in the university office that manages relations between Chinese institutions and the external world and for political science professors, I was a "returned student" who had already passed the more intense scrutiny of another era. By the late 1970s, the Cultural Revolution view of Westerners as spies had already faded considerably, but awkward questions about my relationship to my government had certainly been considered and already answered in ways not detrimental to my research.

Most of my interviews with retired officials were arranged through friends. My purpose was largely exploratory. At the time I began them, my understanding of the issues derived almost exclusively from official published sources, supplemented later by interviews with officials in the departments that implemented the policy. My research questions had yet to be honed. Although I ultimately conducted a larger systematic survey, I was not prepared at the outset to design a questionnaire containing unambiguous, specific items presented in the forced-choice format that facilitates objective coding for quantitative analysis.

Given the exploratory and orienting aims of the interviews, reliability of response was the top priority. More than anything, I needed subjects to provide frank and complete accounts of an event that was very personal and, for most, highly emotional. The thirty-six retired officials I interviewed were a convenience sample. Most interview subjects were known to me personally or had been introduced through friends who knew them. They were the parents of school friends and of friends of friends. The personal connection between respondents and myself, however tenuous, did not guarantee reliability, but my Chinese friends and I believe it enhanced it.

In describing my research to retired officials, I explained that I had read papers and books about retirement policy and met with officials in veteran cadre departments but that I did not think I could understand retirement without listening to them. I asked them to help me understand retirement by giving me a different perspective based on their personal experience. I assured them I would not use their names in anything I made public but would draw on what I had learned from them to shape further research and what I wrote. I refrained from taking notes until a conversation was well under way and a rapport established, often on the basis of a personal story.

Identity and Rapport

If age, experience, and rank incline Chinese officials toward wariness in interviews, retirement inclines them to be forthcoming. Most have plenty of time to spare, like to talk, and are fairly articulate. Not least of all, compared to those with positions to lose, retired officials probably felt less constrained about what they said to me. This higher comfort level may have been enhanced by the fact that I conducted most interviews in the privacy of their homes, their familiar and personal turf. The personal connection, my obvious interest in their story, and my language fluency undoubtedly also inclined them to open up. Yet, if these features of my identity shortened the distance between us, my relative youth and my foreignness created a distance. This was not necessarily detrimental to my purpose: It identified me as a naïve witness, someone truly in need of their help to understand the meaning of Chinese cadre retirement in context.

A colleague in Hong Kong believes my respondents were more comfortable telling their stories to a woman than would have been the case were I male. I have no idea whether this was the case. In interviews with younger officials, my gender did become a factor—but only because it created culturally defined problems of access, described later.

If informal enforcers were to emerge to implement the policy as a norm, younger officials, who had the most to gain from the retirement of their elders, were the most likely candidates. To learn about their perspective, I conducted interviews with seventy-one younger officials, sent from workplaces in nearly every province in China to Peking University to obtain the college-graduate equivalence that would help qualify them for promotion.

My original plan was to interview these officials singly, in my dormitory room. This was rejected as unacceptable by the university. Nearly all of the officials were young men, and it would be "inconvenient" for me, a young foreign woman, to meet with them alone in my room. The proposed solution was to allow me to interview them in groups in a small meeting room. I accepted the change of venue but not the group interviews. What was required here was for university administrators to see the situation in a different framework: to see me as a scholar (not a young foreign woman) and the officials as my interview subjects (not young Chinese men from unsophisticated towns, entrusted to the care of the university authorities). The support of my Chinese research supervisor and other professors in political science was crucial here. They understood my research aims and the potentially inhibiting effect on response of group interviews. They communicated to the university my reasons for requesting individual interviews. Without the help of Chinese political scientists, I believe the university would not ultimately have granted approval for individual interviews.

I had no personal connection with the younger officials I interviewed. They were fairly young and had been away from their workplaces and homes for more than one year. Some remarked on the comparatively relaxed environment at the university. These factors may have contributed to frankness.

Language Fluency: An Essential Asset

The account so far notes only in passing what I consider as my most important access "instrument": language. Without Chinese language fluency, I cannot imagine forming the friendships that ultimately proved so crucial to meeting my main access challenge. Nor can I imagine developing rapport with my interview subjects, especially the older retired officials, without a fluency that put them at ease and reduced the cultural distance between us. Language fluency also gave me credibility, demonstrating a commitment of many years. Of course, in later projects—interviewing Chinese villagers in the countryside, for example—language fluency helped hardly at all, because of dialect.

Ongoing Issues of Access

Much in China has changed since the mid-1980s. Yet, scholarly research remains hostage to political events that affect the overall environment for empirical research. Research requiring access to Chinese as ordinary respondents, especially on issues that the regime defines as sensitive, remains fraught with uncertainty, with less under the control of the researcher than in other sorts of projects. In these circumstances, language and friends, both serious investments of time that demand more commitment than calculation, are invaluable: They open some doors and make tolerable those that remain as yet closed. The Chinese party-state does not view social science research by foreigners benignly. In the preparation of research products, just as it is obviously irresponsible to pander to whatever political correctness prevails on the mainland, it is also irresponsible to forget that when we exit, our Chinese friends remain behind. Moreover, unless we intend never to do further research in China, our "exit" is never really complete. We will return many times over the years. In both these senses, friendships can be constraining. Until the climate for social science research in China changes dramatically, some constraint is a tradeoff for research in which access depends on friends.

Dealing with Difficult Gatekeepers, Vulnerable Populations, and "Hooks" That Go Awry

Michele Tracy Berger

A central issue I explored in my dissertation was how a group of marginal women (former crack cocaine users and sex workers) became politically active after contracting HIV/AIDS.[16] Initially, I was interested in the meanings women assigned to their illicit activities. In the first phase of my fieldwork in Detroit, I decided to concentrate on women who had self-defined problems with crack cocaine and some experience with street-level sex work.

Because I was interviewing women in Detroit who were most often transient, I was required to gain access not only directly to them but also to the various institutions and organizations they passed through during their multiple phases of addiction, recovery, and relapse. This was necessary to understand how they responded to multiple setbacks and assess the kinds of resources that were (or weren't) available to them during these times. These institutions and organizations included a nonprofit women's organization, substance abuse treatment facilities, HIV/AIDS organizations, hospitals, courthouses, homeless shelters, and the Department of Health—all of which had different paths and pitfalls for negotiating access.

I encountered a number of gatekeepers while trying to gain access to respondents. Lawyers, judges, substance abuse and HIV/AIDS counselors, bailiffs, hospital staff, and general human services workers were some of the gatekeepers I met. Gatekeepers often impeded my ability to gain access to this population.

All of the challenging aspects of access in field research are intensified when working with populations engaged in illicit and stigmatized activities such as substance use, theft, and sex work. Thus, my access story highlights both specific issues connected with the challenges of obtaining access to a vulnerable population and generalizable concerns for researchers on the following topics: (1) the importance of a flexible hook, (2) the role of gatekeepers in institutions, and (3) the relationship between identity and rapport.

When the Hook Doesn't Take

The hook I originally used, during the summer of 1994, for gaining access to women while in various institutions and organizations was not an effective one. I was to discover that there were a number of emotionally charged meanings between "crack cocaine use," "women," and "street-level sex work" for most gatekeepers. Gatekeepers often held the attitude that the pharmacological experience of crack cocaine use explained everything about a woman's actions. This attitude often resulted in "the crack made her do it" reasoning. Moreover, although my use of the term "sex work" was grounded in the arguments scholars and activists had advanced in the last two decades, it was definitely the "wrong" term to use for this audience in explaining one aspect of my interest in the women's activities. Most gatekeepers were not familiar with the term, and they often had negative views of women who prostituted. They understood urban prostitution as unpleasant, dangerous, and degrading. Based on my unsuccessful hook, I often got three categories of responses from people who initially refused me access to potential respondents.

Protection, Knowledge, and Authority, and Methods

Gatekeepers, particularly those at substance abuse treatment centers and the nonprofit women's organization, wanted to "protect" respondents from having to discuss troubling or difficult aspects of their lives. I stressed that during the interview respondents would discuss only what they were comfortable with and that I was bound by my consent release to inform a respondent of her right to stop the interview at any time, but these precautions did not allay their concerns.

Gatekeepers often suggested I could get "better and more accurate" information about the women from talking with counselors, social workers, and drug counselors— that is, with *them*. Because of most respondents' heavy drug use and poor educational background, gatekeepers believed the women to be cognitively incoherent and therefore inarticulate about their experiences. Their disdain for the women was palpable.

Although I discussed my methodology at length with gatekeepers (interviews lasted an hour and were open-ended, with a possible longer oral history conducted with some respondents), they often didn't understand the value of listening to "oral history." Some places, such as hospitals and the Department of Health, were familiar with survey research. To many, qualitative methods seemed "risky, individualistic, and unsystematic."

Changing the Hook

So, after almost a complete summer in the field with no institutional access and minimal street access, my hook changed and became "I'm going to discuss with the women how difficult and degrading crack cocaine use, prostitution, and recovery is for them." I retraced my steps with many of the institutions and organizations and was fortunate to get interviews with different gatekeepers. I tried to avoid, if I could, the people whom I had spoken with during the first round of trying to gain access. This meant more telephone and leg work for me, but I wanted to start with a clean slate. Luckily, most of the institutions and organizations had several people working in areas that didn't overlap.

As long as I stressed the idea that the women were "victims" in every respect and downplayed interpretative ambiguity and conflict, many of the gatekeepers were satisfied. I suggested to the gatekeepers that the women's stories would be a confirmation of what researchers and lay people already "knew"—that these women simply had "terrible lives"; they were not in control of their lives and not to blame for their circumstances—nothing more and nothing less. Although I wasn't happy about this strategy, this hook often "fit" with the therapeutic approach that the particular organization was trying to ideologically reinforce, and it worked to provide access to respondents.

A few general lessons can be gleaned from my experience. The first is that a researcher should consider the hidden agendas, ideologies, and culture that shape institutions and organizations. The second is that a hook is better when it is short and simple. Gatekeepers have many other commitments, and most often they won't take the time to understand the minutiae involved in the chosen research topic that a hook represents. Also, if it appears that one's access strategy is not going over well with certain gatekeepers, it's helpful to try to categorize the type of rejection that one receives. Planning ahead to counter or redirect assumptions might be helpful, but a researcher shouldn't be afraid to modify, or completely scrap a hook that isn't working.

Gaining Rapport with the Women

Interestingly enough, although gatekeepers perceived me as strange for wanting to research this population, the women did not perceive me as unusual. They did not ask me to justify myself. Their experience of me was influenced by my blackness, femaleness, education, and age. These social identities mediated the experiences in a way I hadn't expected. They perceived me as a "nice black girl."

The women often remarked that I reminded them of some distant cousin, friend, companion, or other person. This way of explaining and maintaining a familiarity between researcher and researched, in the field, is what others have labeled as "fictive kin" status. This sense of fictive kin status put them at ease and helped them trust me. I often accepted the role and engaged in the performance of "naïve" younger woman/nice girl, because it allowed me to participate in their lives and gave them a forum in which to tell their stories. Additionally, many women of color, particularly African Americans, stated they would not have necessarily talked about their experiences with a white researcher.

Identifying the women as knowledgeable about their own experiences helped facilitate trust and rapport between us. But they did not just talk to me because they trusted me. They also felt that *they* had something to gain by telling me their story. "Setting the record straight" was a prime motivation for many women, those actively using drugs, those in recovery, and those who were HIV-positive. They were very concerned that "outside" people understand the unique challenges in their lives, as different and distinct from "stories" people might encounter about women on crack from the television or movies.

Exiting

How I handled exiting the field still disappoints me. I didn't exit the field in a manner, with the majority of the women or the gatekeepers, that would facilitate easy reentry. For some respondents, their transient lifestyle made it difficult to find them and let them know that I was exiting the field. It has been easier to maintain informal ties with the women in my study who were affiliated with institutions or not in the "life" anymore. While gradually exiting the field, for those women with whom I had deeper relationships, I spent time talking with them about the completion of my project. For about a year after I was officially out of the field, I would call some respondents and ask how they were doing or stop by at various meetings just to say hello. Looking back now, there are several things that I wish did while exiting—for example, showing more appreciation to both respondents and gatekeepers for their time and effort and sending more thank-you letters, books, and other types of resources to gatekeepers.

Courting Minorities in Postwar Bosnia

Paula M. Pickering

For my dissertation, I sought deep access to ordinary individuals who live as minorities in Bosnia to understand their everyday strategies for negotiating relationships with neighbors and colleagues who are members of the majority nation. I used intensive interviewing to hear minorities' narratives in their own terms, narratives that weave perspectives and experiences about interethnic relations. In addition, I conducted participant observation of interethnic interaction in neighborhoods. I sought intimate access to the everyday lives of four local families with whom I lived; I asked them to take me on visits to friends and acquaintances beyond their neighborhoods.[17]

Cultivating Trust

I consider the hooks, strategies for gaining access, and means of developing rapport as interconnected components of a process of cultivating trust. This process began in 1996, when I worked in Bosnia as a human rights officer for an intergovernmental organization. It continued during preliminary field research and is ongoing to this very day. This process involved getting to know the needs, concerns, and cultural expectations of Bosnians. Rent was the most concrete hook I presented to the local families with whom I lived. In a postwar economy like Bosnia's, where unemployment hovers around 40 percent, and even those employed often only irregularly receive an average salary of some 180 U.S. dollars per month, my host families viewed rent as a crucial boost to their financial security. Once living with host families, I attempted to cultivate their trust through repeated and respectful interaction in and around the home. Otherwise, the only specific carrots that I used were limited services that I offered to several local voluntary organizations, whose work and network of contacts warranted my involvement. For one, I translated documents. For another, I taught conversational English. I wanted these small services to contribute something to members of the community from which I was taking. I also believe that these services helped me build rapport, because they fostered a more reciprocal relationship between my "subjects" and me.

In general, I believe that my hosts and NGO activists agreed to assist my work because of a tradition of hospitality, the prospect of benefits that might accrue from gaining a good reputation among foreigners (new sublettors or aid), and their confidence in my commitment to listening and learning in a respectful way. Beyond the financial rewards I offered them, my host families may have consented to participate partly as a diversion from the hardship and tediousness of everyday urban life in Bosnia. One local NGO activist, who is familiar with my previous work in Bosnia, appeared "motivated" by the norm of "helping" and a concern for reputation in connecting me to a host family and some interviewees.

Strategies for Access

Given that many scholars and Bosnian minorities considered the war to be about eliminating minorities, I foresaw that access would be difficult. Not even preliminary fieldwork, however, prepared me for the exceedingly high levels of interpersonal mistrust that I encountered. One minority friend who denied me an interview warned me, "Here in Bosnia, even breathing is political," and thus controversial and dangerous.

My primary strategies for gaining access were living with minorities and participating in their everyday lives (for participant observation) and snowball sampling (for intensive interviewing). For participant observation, I rented a room in a minority family's apartment for three months; this schedule allowed me to live with two different families in separate neighborhoods in each of two Bosnian cities. To identify potential minority host families, I asked minorities with whom I had previously worked for suggestions. I told Bosnians that I was trying to understand the problems that ordinary people encountered in coping with their everyday lives—particularly their relationships with their neighbors—in the difficult postwar period. I promised to listen intently, commenting that many foreigners spent too much time talking with politicians and too little time listening to ordinary Bosnians, whose concerns were important for building a sustainable peace.

I did not approach minority neighbors and activists for intensive interviews until I had conducted sustained "soaking and poking" and had repeatedly interacted with them over several months. I felt they would consider discussing personal experiences only after having an opportunity to judge my trustworthiness. In attempting to overcome a postconflict atmosphere of intense distrust, I spent considerable time with Bosnians expressing interest in activities and concerns that stretched beyond my research focus. Once I participated in a minority NGO's workshop on women in the media; I sat another evening for four hours with neighborhood women discussing medicinal herbs.

Some—those in the direst circumstances—appeared more approachable than others. One Serb single mother who had fled during the war and returned to Sarajevo afterward with her teenage son spent several hours one morning in a café sharing her personal experiences. She confessed that she was thankful for merely a place to sit so that she could give her son some privacy in the single room they subletted from an acquaintance. Her plight made her more willing to talk. In contrast, some slightly less desperate Bosnians who realized that I had nothing "concrete," like a job, to offer them were understandably hesitant to delve into sensitive interethnic issues.

My in-depth strategy for access to ordinary persons helped me deal with the unforeseen obstacles presented by the eruption midway into my research of war in neighboring Kosovo. NATO bombing and violence by Serb extremists heightened anti-Serb sentiment in Muslim-majority Bosnia where I worked and anti-American sentiment among Serbs, making it more difficult to recruit new Serb respondents.

Luckily, I had been working with local human rights NGOs assisting Serbs and socializing with a group of Serb families for months. As a result, I had already achieved a level of rapport that enabled me to continue participating actively in neighborhoods populated by Serbs and to conduct interviews.

I used a different strategy—volunteering—to get to know a few NGOs' minority members. To gain access to one minority NGO's clients, I agreed to an activist's suggestion that I follow closely several cases on which the NGO had provided free legal advice. Furthermore, at the request of the minority plaintiff, I observed a hearing. This experience provided an intimate look at interaction between a minority and majority officials, and it even helped bring about progress in the case, though it jeopardized my impartiality.

Impact of Identity

This is one illustration of how my identity affected informants' behavior. One of my primary methods was ethnographic participant observation. While I knew I could never climb out of my own identity and become a Bosnian, I felt that gaining deep understanding and access demanded that I convincingly convey respect for Bosnian traditions and experiences and not call attention to my foreignness. One Bosnian friend described me as "part American and part Bosnian." Through my observation of Bosnian culture, discussions with other investigators, and attention to the way Bosnians treated me, I estimate that many Bosnians considered me to be a "Western female student keenly interested in people in Bosnia and in reconstruction of multiethnicity there."

In a tense environment and one where Bosnians believe that Westerners want locals to express cultural tolerance, I found participant observation to reveal more about interethnic relations than a one-shot interview. Participant observation allowed me to build rapport over a period of time and to observe actions in a multitude of contexts and with a variety of people. This made it impossible for locals to tailor constantly their behavior to match Western hopes. Though most Bosnians assumed my views were infected by the bias of American policy, they did not impose on me the prejudices that Bosnians would attach to someone with roots in one of Bosnia's ethnic groups. I endeavored to make the most of this relative neutrality by conducting interviews without a translator.

I found that women and older persons were more willing to discuss their interethnic experiences than were others. I attributed this partly due to gender roles and partly to the connection between their current interethnic relationships and their wartime experiences. I found it difficult to talk with men of fighting age, whose wartime experiences were generally horrifying. Men beyond fighting age were more forthcoming. One young male minority who had fought for the Muslim- (majority-)

led army declined an interview and hoped that I could provide protection to male respondents. This rejection could not be explained merely by intimacy with horror, because several women shared their experiences with rape, while some Bosnian men retold war stories to male investigators. Instead, I believe gender roles in Bosnia made it unlikely that young men would share their feelings with women.

Building Rapport

In cultivating rapport and building trust, I attempted to respect Bosnians and convey passionate concern about my research problems and their practical impact on peoples. On several occasions, informants and colleagues mentioned that my early communication of enthusiasm influenced their willingness to speak for me. I attempted to be a good listener, which persons recently experiencing war particularly appreciate. Some Bosnians considered my living with local families and knowledge of the local language as demonstrating my willingness to learn. Reflecting on my interview questions, a few Bosnians commented that they were impressed by my knowledge of Bosnia and my unwillingness to settle for superficial responses. To help meet some Bosnians' practical needs, I offered tiny favors, such as connecting them to humanitarian organizations or giving them rides.

Access Achieved

One indication of the access I achieved was the amount of time—sometimes four hours—some Bosnians spent with me discussing highly sensitive issues. On a more worrisome note, other signs included the level of emotion that some of my subjects expressed, from sobbing during an interview to breaking out in a rash just after one. My use of multiple methods exposed divergence between *opinions* expressed in interviews or coffee visits and *actions* that I witnessed as part of a neighborhood community. For instance, one minority informant repeatedly told me, "I've never paid attention to ethnicity." But as I observed her neighborhood interactions, I noticed that she considered her new neighbors of the majority group as disrespectful and avoided them. In other cases, I noticed a progression in the level of trust. Toward the end of my work as a volunteer, a minority NGO critical of interference by Westerners sought my opinion during a workshop. After living with one minority woman for two months, I was invited to intimate family gatherings.

Disengaging

Because I lived in four different neighborhoods within Bosnia, I had to disengage from Bosnians five times—once partly in each locality and then when I left the country. During my stay in Bosnia, I continued to visit former neighbors and activists. I was not always able, however, to live up to my goal of properly disengaging in the end. In my second site, I missed teaching my last English class and thus my planned "good-bye" session because of overscheduling and illness. I tried to apologize to my students in a letter. Now back in the United States, I have written notes and sent photos to informants and subjects; I also talk on the phone with my closest friends there. I will never completely disengage from the Bosnians who, though struggling to survive, brought me into their homes and lives. These people, their stories, and our experiences enrich virtually every day of my life.

Notes

1. Ann Cornelisen, *Women of the Shadows* (Boston: Little, Brown, 1976).

2. Stoller, *The Taste of Ethnographic Things*.

3. Spradley, *The Ethnographic Interview*, 25.

4. William Foote Whyte, *Street Corner Society* (Chicago: University of Chicago Press, 1943).

5. Elliot Liebow, *Tally's Corner: A Study of Negro Streetcorner Men* (Boston: Little, Brown, 1967).

6. Liebow, *Tally's Corner*, 242.

7. Susan Eckstein, *The Poverty of Revolution: The State and the Urban Poor in Mexico* (Princeton, N.J.: Princeton University Press, 1977), 241.

8. Michael McCall, "Who and Where Are the Artists?" in *Fieldwork Experience, Qualitative Approaches to Social Research*, ed. William B. Shaffier, Robert A. Stebbins, and Allan Turowetz (New York: St. Martin's, 1980), 146.

9. Studs Terkel, *Working* (New York: Ballantine, 1972), xxv.

10. Here are a few examples of such researchers' access stories: Jonathan Rieder, *Canarsie: The Jews and Italians of Brooklyn against Liberalism* (Cambridge, Mass.: Harvard University Press, 1985), 6–9; Fenno, *Homestyle*, 279; Liebow, *Tally's Corner*, 233–56; Eckstein, *The Poverty of Revolution*, 221–46.

11. Spradley, *The Ethnographic Interview*, 45–46.

12. Kathryn Edin and Laura Lein, *Making Ends Meet* (New York: Russell Sage Foundation, 1997)

13. Fenno, *Homestyle*, 264.

14. Ann Chih Lin, Amaney Jamal, and Abigail J. Stewart, "Patriarchy, Connection, and Individualism: Immigration and the Experience of Gender in Arab Immigrant Families," unpublished manuscript.

15. Melanie Manion, *Retirement of Revolutionaries in China: Public Policies, Social Norms, Private Interests* (Princeton, N.J.: Princeton University Press, 1993).

16. Michele Tracy Berger, "Advocates, Activists and Helpers: Multiple Expressions of Activism by HIV-Positive African-American Women in Detroit," *Womanist Theory and Research: A Journal of Womanist and Feminist of Color Scholarship and Art*, 3 (2001/2002): 21–28; and Michele Tracy Berger, "'Quit Stigmatizing Us': The Role of Stigma in the Process of Political Participation among African-American Women with HIV/AIDS," in *African-American Women in Politics: A Reader*, ed. Rose Harris, unpublished manuscript.

17. Paula Pickering, "The Choices Minorities Make about Diversity: Migration and Negotiation in Postwar Bosnia-Hercegovina," Ph.D. diss., University of Michigan, 2001; Paula Pickering, "Strategies Minorities Use to Negotiate with the Majority in Post-War Bosnia-Herzegovina," in *New Approaches to Balkan Studies,* ed. Dimitris Keridis (New York: Brassey's, 2001).

Gaining Access for Interviewing   7

THE STORIES IN THIS CHAPTER address challenges faced by those who seek access to conduct interviews. Researchers may desire access to conduct interviews of individuals who are part of a single organization—congresspeople, Supreme Court justices and clerks, hospital board members, or those in similar organizational contexts who do not necessarily belong to the same organization or group but are linked through informal networks—psychiatrists, court litigants, abortion activists.[1] The latter context bears considerable similarity to the situation addressed in the previous section, finding informants who are not connected by a common organizational link. Because of this similarity, we place these stories first as a partial segue between this and the previous chapter.

In the first of the access stories below, Garcia-Johnson describes her efforts to gain access to people related to the chemical industries in Brazil, Mexico, and the United States. She not only interviewed people in different countries who had no connection to one another but also interviewed people who had entirely different perspectives on the chemical industry. Some of her informants are employees of multinational corporations in the chemical industry; others are critics of these organizations. In the second story, Jelen relates his efforts to gain access to the clergy of different denominations of Christian churches. While some of these people knew each other, many did not.

Though gaining access for these researchers is similar in many ways to the stories in the previous chapter, the organizational context is nonetheless an important element in their work. What all of Garcia-Johnson's informants had in common was the chemical industry. She needed to learn about this industry to be able to talk with them. She also learned more about this fundamentally organizational phenomenon through her interviews. The church and the relationship between the clergy and the parishioners served a similar role in Jelen's work. In this sense, these stories are similar to the other two access stories in this chapter in which the researchers studied aspects of a single organization—in one case, the World Bank; in the other case, a university hospital.

Doing Interviews and Gaining Information

Face-to-face interviews, as a format, may permit the researchers to target specific issues, get questions answered, and test hypotheses.[2] Just having physical access to individuals, the necessary first step, however, does not mean that interviews will allow access to the information that the researcher needs. Often to get the information, the interviewers must motivate informants to answer questions posed to them both fully and accurately.[3]

If researchers take steps to prepare themselves adequately before beginning fieldwork, it is possible to increase the amount of information communicated during the interview. This is important in conducting elite interviews, in which the interviewee has specialized knowledge and very little time to impart it.[4] Other people or other documents could also provide much of the nonspecialized information that such interviewees could provide. Therefore, the researcher wants to ask only for the specialized knowledge that can only be provided by this person. Researchers who have prepared themselves by doing homework in the area are more likely to be able to take advantage of the particular information the informant has to offer.

Questions that show particularized knowledge of the area also suggest that the researcher should be taken seriously. One researcher studying psychiatrists who were also public figures had had little difficulty getting psychiatrists to agree to do interviews. He discovered quickly, however, that his informants revealed little that extended his knowledge beyond the information he had gathered while doing preparatory work prior to going into the field.[5] Preparatory work was thus crucial because it allowed the researcher to learn that his respondents were being superficial. The researcher used this knowledge by pointing out informants' minor factual errors, or brief memory lapses—when they confused a date, for instance. Doing this signaled to the informant that he or she should take the project seriously. The researcher believes that this was an important resource in gaining access to the desired information.[6]

Though highlighting his knowledge worked for the researcher cited here, such aggressive tactics may not work in all contexts. Specialized knowledge can be a double-edged sword, and it is important to recognize the disadvantages if one is to use knowledge effectively to facilitate access. Displaying too much knowledge can get in the way of showing that you have things to learn and thus cause informants to provide less information. If you show too much knowledge, interviewees may feel alienated. Your informants may wonder what information they are adding and whether the researcher is wasting their time. It can give the interviewees the impression that you already know the answers to your questions and that you are wasting both their time and yours. Learning how to display simultaneously that you are serious, that you have done your homework, and that you really want to learn from your interviews is a stance that takes some practice.

There are, of course, other indicators that you should be taken seriously as a researcher and that you take your interviewee seriously. Sometimes these are displayed through physical presentation, such as the type of clothes worn. The researcher's previous profession, institutional affiliation, reputation, or even the social ties may also provide signals that he or she should be taken seriously. In some cases, this may happen before the interview takes place, as the person who grants initial access in an organization passes the message along to others that the research should be taken seriously. This experience happened to one researcher conducting interviews of U.S. Supreme Court clerks in Washington, D.C. He began to explain his project to an informant with whom he was setting up an interview. No sooner had he begun when the informant interjected, "I know who you are. You don't do something like this in Washington without everybody knowing about it. I've already heard that you are okay."[7] In this case, the researcher's reputation and trustworthiness had been established by persons previously interviewed, thereby eliminating the need for the informant to worry about disclosing information.

If one's credentials or reputation have not preceded the researcher and he or she is not gaining access to the information desired, it is possible to develop rapport by briefly raising a common experience, common identity, or even a social tie that the researcher and informant share. Establishing a connection in this way may not only foster trust between the informant and researcher but also increase the informant's desire to do all he or she can to help. One researcher who was studying hospital board members had difficulty, as she called it, "penetrating beyond what anyone could have read in the hospital's annual report."[8] Though the researcher had been able to get her foot in the door, interviews were shorter than she wished and did not provide anything more than what would ordinarily be disclosed to the public. All of this changed when by chance during one interview the informant discovered that he knew a member of the researcher's family. The rest of the interview was dramatically different, the researcher insisted, from all of her previous data. The sudden richness of her data signaled the importance of the researcher's identity to the access she received. She maintained, "Who I was or was perceived to be influenced the information to which I would be given access. The management of my identity thus became an important aspect of my research strategy."[9]

Developing Rapport with Multiple Individuals

A crucial access issue for researchers who choose to interview is for them to obtain access to individuals, often to many individuals. Access to many individuals provides different perspectives on the issue of concern to the researcher. Rapport, however, is still essential, because without rapport it can happen that none of the individuals will provide the insights that the researchers need. A most dramatic story of this sort is told by Paul Stoller in his book *The Taste of Ethnographic Things*,[10] in which he relates how every single person that he interviewed in an entire village lied to him in response to a straightforward query: the number of languages they spoke. While such dramatic and verifiable deception may be unusual, less clear deception may be even more difficult for a researcher to deal with, casting doubt on their entire research project in ways that they have little ability to control.

Rapport is not something that just develops between the researcher and informant. All of the stories in this chapter and many in the rest of the book emphasize the importance of paying close attention to what works in the context in which one is seeking access. Showing up regularly for church services helps build trust among clergy; that strategy may not have worked in another institutional setting. Miller-Adams and Myers used knowledge of the context of the World Bank to facilitate access. Because they knew the World Bank to be a closed place to outsiders, including academics (because of past critical reports), they followed certain procedures—using note taking rather than tape recording and informing certain people at the World Bank that the research would still be conducted regardless of their specific input. By doing this, they were able to create more incentive for people who worked there to tell their side of the story, and they were able to draw on their different yet compelling institutional identities.

Sometimes the organizational context considerably eases access to the interviewees. This is illustrated in the last story in this chapter by Wrzesniewski, Dutton, and Debebe. Finding the people to interview and scheduling the interviews would have been exceedingly difficult in this context had it not been for the intervention of "Grace," a midlevel manager who took an interest in the research project and facilitated the interviewing process. This story represents the opposite end of the spectrum from elite interviewing. The hospital cleaners studied had very little control over their time and would almost surely not have had the time to talk with the researchers if the interviews had not been sanctioned and facilitated through hierarchical channels. The researchers were lucky to find a person who was willing to serve this function for them, and, clearly, finding her is a major part of their access story. They were not the only researchers to have found people who enabled their research without asking anything in return. Such stories remind us that goodwill is also a part of the research process and that accepting gifts is part of the relationships on which we rely.

Accessing Business, Government, and Nongovernmental Organization Actors in Mexico and Brazil

Ronie Garcia-Johnson

The question I explored in my dissertation, which was revised and eventually published as *Exporting Environmentalism: U.S. Multinational Chemical Corporations in Brazil and Mexico* (MIT Press, 2000), concerned the transnational diffusion of environmental ideology. I was particularly interested in business actors working in multinational corporations. How did business people from industrialized countries share their environmental ideas and values with those in industrializing ones? When, why, and how did business people in industrializing countries accept or reject incoming ideology? What effects did this ideology have on environmental policies, on environmental movements, and on the environment?

I focused my research on multinational corporations in the chemical industries of the United States, Brazil, and Mexico and determined that I needed to speak with company executives and managers, trade association representatives, government officials, environmental activists, and scholars in the three countries. Beyond the language barrier (which I resolved by studying Brazilian Portuguese for a year), this international research project posed a few problems. First, I had no money for travel; airfare and accommodations for research in Brazil were particularly expensive. I applied for grants and secured funding for pilot and primary research from the Latin American and Caribbean Studies Program and the Center for International Business Education at the University of Michigan, and the Institute for the Study of World Politics in Washington, D.C. The second problem was that, as the mother of a young daughter, I had limited time to spend away in the field. I planned a six-week trip (three weeks in Mexico and three in Brazil) in 1996 and then another two trips, with three weeks in each country, in 1997, in part so that I would not have to be away from her for months at a time.

Finally, I had no contacts in the chemical industry and no academic or government contacts in Brazil or Mexico; I had to network to develop a list of contacts. I visited professors at my graduate and undergraduate institutions, sent e-mail messages to Brazilian and Mexican student groups, and recorded the names and numbers of alumni from my universities in Brazil and Mexico. One professor provided the name of just one business executive, who in turn gave me the names and numbers of his colleagues working in company subsidiaries in Brazil and Mexico. I called these two individuals from the United States, making appointments to interview them when I arrived. These were the only appointments I had before I left the United States for my initial pilot work and fieldwork.

Accessing Individuals in Mexico and Brazil

Despite the work I had done to prepare for my initial trip to Mexico, my arrival in Mexico City was an overwhelming experience. As I had no institutional support within the country, there was no one to greet me or to guide me. While I am Mexican American and do not stand out in Mexico, my formal Spanish gave me away as a foreigner. The polluted streets, the chaotic traffic, and the invasive stares of men on the streets intensified my anxiety. I found an inexpensive hotel, locked myself in my room, and cried. What had I been thinking, coming to Mexico with just the names and numbers of a few strangers? How would I get anyone to speak with me, let alone get around such a complex city?

The next morning I forced myself to pick up the telephone to contact the people on my list and others I found in the many telephone books for the city. It took a lot of persistence to schedule just one interview. I had to learn how to use the telephone cards, as well as proper telephone etiquette. When I finally managed to reach a contact, I explained in Spanish what I wanted to know, that I had just a few weeks in Mexico, and that I wanted just one hour of their time for an interview. When my list or the telephone books failed me, I went exploring to track down interviewees. No one flatly refused to see me.

The scholars I met on my first visits to Brazil and Mexico were supportive and provided government and NGO contacts more than industrial ones. The NGO representatives were also very helpful, leading me to their peers. However, I was most enthusiastically accommodated by people in the business community. Some of these people spent hours with me or went out of their way to see me. Once I met and interviewed these executives, managers, or trade association representatives, they each provided me with more names and telephone numbers. I quickly turned the two multinational corporation contacts I had before I left the United States into over twenty interviews with the business actors who had previously seemed most remote to me.

I did not provide a hook to convince people to speak with me—the hook had been created by the chemical industry. Chemical industry representatives in Mexico and Brazil seemed eager to talk about their activities, perhaps because they wanted acknowledgment for their efforts to "green" their operations. NGO leaders were also very eager to talk about environmentalism in Brazil and Mexico and about the public relations aspects of greening efforts. Government officials were the most difficult to contact, especially in Mexico, and they did not seem especially eager to discuss the problems of regulating the chemical industry.

Developing Rapport

The travel guides I read to prepare for my first visits advised me to look like the people in the country I was visiting. I thought that fitting in made good sense on the street and in interview settings. Many of the professional women I saw in both Brazil and Mexico were carefully dressed in coordinated outfits. To gain the initial respect of receptionists and interviewees alike, I made sure to look as polished as these Mexican and Brazilian professional women when I visited industry offices. I felt more comfortable looking like a graduate student on a budget when I spoke with scholars and NGO activists. But wherever I went during my first visits to Brazil and Mexico, I was presented with business cards. During my first trip, I sheepishly wrote my contact information on sheets of notebook paper, but I had business cards made for my second visits.

There were some other things about me that I could not change that helped me develop rapport, especially in my interviews with business people. First, I was a girlish-looking woman. I met mostly with men. While they were very polite and respectful, many commented on my youth and the fact that I was working on a doctoral degree (wasn't I too young for that?), and almost all suggested that I was vulnerable on the dangerous streets of the city. Many also commented that I looked Mexican or Brazilian ("just like a Brazilian girl") and asked me about my Spanish last name. This suggests to me that these men did not initially feel threatened by me; they seemed to feel comfortable helping me.

Another factor working in my favor as I sought access was the fact that I was American and that I had attended well-known universities. As many executives had spent time in the United States, we could chat about familiar places. Many of my interviewees seemed pleased to see an American learning and speaking their language. There is so much emphasis, in Mexico and Brazil, on the importance of learning English that most understood how I felt when I stumbled over an irregular verb, and they gracefully corrected me. A couple of my interviewees insisted on speaking English during the interviews so they could practice with me! Just talking about whether we would conduct the interview in Spanish, Portuguese, English, or some combination helped develop rapport.

Yet perhaps the single most important way of developing rapport was to communicate the genuine fascination I had for the work of my interviewees. They seemed to enjoy knowing that their everyday activities were interesting to a foreign scholar. They were delighted to teach me what they knew so well.

Issues of Safety

I was nervous about traveling alone in two of the largest cities in the world and was determined to appear as inconspicuous as possible. Each day, as I moved by foot or public transportation from my hotel in the deteriorated center of the city to the posh new industrial sectors, I would slowly change my own appearance. I emerged from my hotel with a modest coat over my suit and wore tennis shoes or sandals right up to the doors of the office buildings, where I put on business shoes. I bought a cheap plastic market bag to hold and hide my old coat, extra shoes, and invaluable notes.

Near the end of my first trip to Mexico, I realized that men would not follow or whistle at apparently pregnant women. On my second trip, when I felt vulnerable walking down the street on the fringes of the city, I knotted my sweater around my waist and buttoned up my coat over the bulge. Passing men no longer seemed to notice me. And each country was different: While in Mexico City, bare arms attracted attention; in Rio de Janeiro, I felt silly with sleeves.

Once I opened my mouth, I was exposed (especially in Brazil) and was asked where I was from. On the street in depressed sections of the city, being an American was not an asset (as interviewees and other contacts constantly reminded me). When strangers noted my accent and began asking questions that made me uncomfortable, I mumbled that I was from some other country and crossed the street. I rode the subways rather than getting into a taxi with a strange driver. I always tried to walk as though I knew exactly where I was going and kept my maps out of sight. When I had to ask for directions, I tried to ask people in family groups.

I blew my cover once on a bus in Rio de Janeiro. I was feeling proud of my ability to blend in and get around like any *carioca* when I felt something tickle my underarm. When the tickle did not go away, I realized that one of my worst travel nightmares had come true: A yellow beetle the size of a quarter was under my shirt, working its way across my chest. Tearing at my blouse to free my uninvited guest, I jumped up in my seat and upset the stout, dignified woman sitting next to me. "O que é?" she screamed, jumping up and down with me. I broke my silence in English, Spanish, and then finally, correctly, in Portuguese. "A bug! Un insecto! Um insecto!" Everyone on the bus laughed, and even though I was hysterically laughing too, I changed buses. I had blown my cover.

Maintaining Access

I was careful to thank my contacts and interviewees after my first visits by sending typed thank-you notes from the United States. I did this more to express my sincere appreciation rather than to secure a second interview. But this approach made me feel more comfortable contacting some of them in preparation for my second trips by fax and e-mail and thus helped me maintain access. I brought some printed notes with university themes (my department did not give us stationery) to send from within Brazil and Mexico on my second trips.

I have developed lasting relationships with some of my dissertation contacts, and these relationships have led to exciting new projects. Perhaps more important, these relationships allow policymakers, business leaders, and other scholars access to me and to my work in an ongoing process of collaboration. After taking from so many, I am now giving something back.

Rendering unto Caesar:
Gaining Access to Local Religious Leaders

Ted G. Jelen

The main purpose of my research was to determine why some American church members apply their religious beliefs to their political attitudes and behavior, while others appear to compartmentalize the secular and the sacred. My interest in religion and politics began in the early 1980s, as leaders of the Christian Right (a phenomenon primarily associated with evangelical Protestantism) and the Catholic Church became increasingly vocal and active in American political life. Despite this elite-level activity, relationships between political attitudes and religious affiliations and practices seemed generally weak or inconsistent among the laity. These findings caused me to wonder about the role of the local congregations and pastors in facilitating or inhibiting political learning.[11]

Gaining Initial Access

At the time I conducted this research, I was employed as a professor at Illinois Benedictine College, a Catholic institution in suburban Chicago. The research site I chose was Putnam County, Indiana. This proved to be a fortunate decision, because I was able to enlist the assistance of two professors of religious studies at DePauw University, who happened also to be ordained ministers. My faculty informants at DePauw were most helpful in gaining initial access to virtually all of the congregations in my sample. Based on their advice, I sent each pastor a custom-written letter, briefly explaining my position and my project in general terms. Since one of the substantive findings of my research was that there was considerable interdenominational conflict in Putnam County, the assistance of religious and academic mentors who were familiar with the local religious scene was quite fortuitous.

Only one minister responded to my initial mailing. Thus, I sent each a follow-up letter and contacted each by telephone a week later. In these telephone conversations, I simply informed the pastors that I would be in town on a particular date and requested permission to visit them and discuss this project. While several of the pastors were somewhat reluctant, all but one were willing to allow me to make my case in person, and most seemed impressed that I was willing to travel some distance to do so.

Closing the Deal

The reactions to my initial personal visits to the pastors (fifteen in all) were quite varied. The more conservative, evangelical, fundamentalist, or Pentecostal ministers received me with a friendly, yet puzzled, curiosity. I encountered questions such as "Why would anyone want to write a book about us?" Once this hurdle was cleared, the ministers were generally quite willing to help.

Among this group of theological conservatives, I encountered no overt discrimination. However, my affiliation with a Catholic institution and my own nominal Catholicism was an occasional source of tension, or, more often, curiosity. On two occasions, I was asked whether I could "really speak Latin," and I demonstrated my feeble prowess to several uncritical, but impressed, audiences. One person, who apparently believed that Roman Catholics were generally recent immigrants into the United States, expressed surprise that I spoke English so well.

The reactions of the mainline pastors were quite different. These ministers were typically substantially more educated then their evangelical counterparts and had no difficulty grasping the purpose of the research. Many of these saw an intimate connection between religion and politics and were often eager to share their insights with me. The reservations I encountered among the theological liberals were of two types. First, several were fearful of the purposes to which I might put the results of the study and were concerned that I might cast their responses in a negative light. In these instances, my connection with a Catholic institution (an occasional barrier in the evangelical community) proved to be an asset. Second, several of these churches were organized quite democratically, and the minister did not have the authority to agree to participate in the study on his own. I was thus required to "sweat out" several board meetings, and I actually attended one to explain who I was and what I was doing. Thus, among the more theologically liberal members of my clergy sample, my status as a Catholic was not problematic, but my status as an academic was a source of suspicion. Perhaps surprisingly, these diverse reservations had little impact on the interviews that followed. Once the initial resistance was overcome, all respondents were extremely cooperative.

In the one Catholic parish in Putnam County, access was simply no problem. The pastor had been trained in the Benedictine order, and a letter from the abbot of St. Procopius Abbey (which operates Illinois Benedictine College) was all that was required to enlist Father John's complete and enthusiastic cooperation.

Establishing Rapport

Establishing rapport with the pastors proved rather easy, despite my determined efforts to undermine my own efforts. My success in this endeavor suggests that simple luck is a badly underappreciated research tool.

The reason that luck was required for me to complete this project was that I had initially committed the most basic error a researcher can commit: I "knew" in advance what I would find and set out to confirm my convictions. My luck consisted of the fact that my first two respondents, who represented very different educational and theological backgrounds, took me to task for making my expectations so clear. In one case, I was convinced that anticommunism was an essential part of evangelical theology (this research was conducted just before the destruction of the Berlin Wall and the fall of the Soviet Union), and I repeatedly pressed a Pentecostal minister for a theological reaction to communism. Since I was not satisfied with his initial reaction that "it [communism] seemed like a good idea, but it just didn't work," I cross-examined him rather intensely. After an uncomfortably long pause, he looked directly at me and said, "You can ask that question as many times as you want and as many ways as you want. The answer isn't going to change." Chagrined, it occurred to me that perhaps I should be quiet and listen to the person whom I was interviewing.

I was extremely fortunate to have this rather embarrassing experience early in my research. After this, I attempted to assume the role of student in my interviews and would deliberately ask apparently naïve questions. Since an important aspect of the ministerial role is instruction in the faith, this was a very familiar setting for most of them. Several of my respondents told me extremely personal things, many of which were not relevant to my research or appropriate for public consumption. For example, one Presbyterian minister's church was located in a community that by local reputation was a center of Ku Klux Klan activity. In our conversation, he chastised himself for his failure to confront the racism in his all-white congregation. He told me that "sometimes, I feel like the gutless wonder, but I just don't feel I can do this. I'm afraid that people will leave." This statement tends to confirm an observation usually credited to Martin Luther King, who suggested that the most segregated hour in America was between 11:00 A.M. and noon on Sunday morning. My experience certainly confirmed King's insight: Only two of my fifteen congregations exhibited any racial diversity at all, and that consisted of one family of color per congregation.

Second Wave

Having gained access to the minister, the next task was to sell the survey to the congregation. In some instances, the pastor either endorsed me from the pulpit (I distributed the surveys at Sunday services, with a self-addressed stamped envelope) or invited me to speak to the congregation. One of my tasks during my long interviews with the clergy was to assess the pastor's enthusiasm for the project. If he did not seem actively supportive, I would delay my distribution of the questionnaires until I had attended several services, Sunday school classes, and church socials. I was apparently less threatening after members of the congregation had seen me chatting with the minister, playing with their children, and enthusiastically munching coffee cake. In establishing rapport with the congregation, I seemed rather successful. The response rate varied enormously from congregation to congregation, but, in my judgment, this variation was mostly the result of differential levels of education on the part of the laity. The response rate ranged from 74 percent in an Episcopalian church (which many members of the university community attended) to 14 percent from a National Baptist congregation (which had a much more working-class membership). My reception in the latter church was extremely friendly, and I was invited to return on several occasions.

Exiting

For a variety of reasons, it seemed important to me not to terminate abruptly my relationships with these people once I had gathered my data. I would typically make another visit several weeks after distributing the questionnaires. On several occasions, I had the opportunity to provide (and to receive) feedback from my respondents. Several of the ministers took me up on my offer to provide the "results" of the survey, and I provided a set of marginal distributions from the survey from the entire sample and from the particular congregation in question. I also was invited by the ministers of two of the mainline congregations to give a talk on my study to Sunday school classes. This proved to be a priceless opportunity to check my impressions and findings against the perceptions of the people whose beliefs I was investigating.

As a frequent visitor to Putnam County, I made occasional visits to each church over the eighteen months following my data collection. Having experienced the hospitality of these clergy and church members so directly, I felt it necessary to withdraw gradually from the community.

Breaking into the Bank: The Challenge of Gaining Meaningful Access to the World Bank

Michelle Miller-Adams and Charles T. Myers

We are two individuals who have gained access to the World Bank to conduct our research. While our interests differed, we both needed to go beyond the organization's official publications and pronouncements to carry out our research projects. As a result, we required a relatively high degree of access to World Bank staff and management.

Miller-Adams: My research focused on how the external environment and internal culture of the World Bank have shaped its evolution, a question I explore through case studies of three new agendas addressed by the organization in recent years.[12] I needed access to staff working in the three areas, senior officials who could provide insight into how these new activities fit into the bank's overall mission, and outside observers and partners of the bank. I also needed to understand the internal workings of the organization and the background and training of its staff and managers.

Myers: In my research project, I wanted to determine why the bank developed programs to promote improved governance in developing countries, a subject it had previously largely shunned.[13] I was interested in learning why the bank had developed the new programs, how it was carrying out these programs, how well they were working, and how they affected the bank's other activities. Because I was seeking information about the bank that went beyond published statements, staff would need to have a degree of confidence in me and a willingness to talk.

A number of factors make gaining access to the World Bank particularly difficult. First, the bank is enormous—a sprawling bureaucracy of close to ten thousand staff members, with field offices around the world. Its scale, diverse activities, and hierarchical structure mean that internal communication is a challenge and researchers are limited in how comprehensive a view of the organization they can obtain. Second, the bank has a distinct organizational culture. Although it employs people of many nationalities, most staff members share a common background based in economics or finance. While it is not necessary to be part of this culture to gain access, it is easier to secure the cooperation of staff and management if one is able to speak the language of the organization.

Third, the World Bank has a well-deserved reputation for being secretive. With few exceptions, the presumption is that information will be shared on a "need to know" basis, and the researcher must make clear the reasons why he or she is asking for answers. In part, the closed character of the World Bank is due to the fact that it is not only a development organization but also a lending institution. As at other financial institutions, the details of negotiations and loan agreements are confidential. Many countries with which the bank deals do not have traditions of openness and do not want the information they supply to the bank made available to the public. This stance can pose a serious obstacle if the researcher wants to observe negotiations or write about them in anything more than a generic way.

But the World Bank's emphasis on secrecy goes beyond concern for its borrowers. The organization has been subject to harsh criticism, and many employees and managers are wary of outsiders. In recent years, the bank has opened up to some extent. Far more documentation is available to the public, and staff members feel somewhat freer to talk with outsiders. But despite the greater openness, management still wants to project a certain image and send a unified message about bank policy. Current leaders have made clear that they do not want staff to criticize bank policy to outsiders, and staff may be reluctant to discuss bank policies negatively for fear of internal retribution or misinterpretation. This is particularly a problem in a climate of uncertainty, such as when the bank has new leadership or is being reorganized. For these reasons, it is unrealistic to expect many bank staff members to depart from the company line. Yet candid insights and valuable information may still be forthcoming, depending on the access and interview strategies employed.

Gaining Access: Two Approaches

Our experience in gaining access to the World Bank suggests that one's approach may depend in part on one's prior experience with, and connections to, the organization.

Myers: I had no entrée to the bank. I simply came up with a list of people I wanted to interview by surveying bank publications on the topic of my research. In an initial letter, I explained the nature of my project, whether I had been referred to them (and by whom), and what it was about their role at the bank that led to my interest in speaking with them. Sometimes people were willing to talk to me; sometimes they referred me to others. Bank staff members are very busy and often travel for extended periods, so working with their schedules was a challenge, but on the whole I found people receptive to at least an initial interview. My hook was straightforward and focused on my research. I stated the question I was interested in and why I thought they might be able to help me with it. Sometimes I mentioned a particular project they had worked on or a report to which they had contributed. I made clear in the wording of my letter that I wanted to look objectively at the bank's work and did not come with a preconceived agenda. I also included a bit about my background, such as the fact that I had practiced law, to enhance my credibility.

Without a sponsor at the bank, I did not get access to the most senior people, although I was able to speak with upper- and midlevel staff, such as project directors and policy advisers, who often have the most specific information and the longest institutional memories among bank employees. I found that people in somewhat more obscure offices were generally willing to meet and were often flattered that someone wanted to see them.

Miller-Adams: During the mid-1980s, I had spent several years following the World Bank on behalf of a major investment bank. As a result, I was able to present myself as something of an insider who understood what the bank was about, had studied it over time, and knew some of its higher-level staff. I relied on these contacts to help me identify others with whom I should speak. The people I contacted generally cooperated, first, because I almost always used the name of one of their colleagues as a reference and, second, because I made clear that the research would be going ahead with or without their input. This created an incentive for people to help me improve the quality of my information and the validity of my findings.

Like Chuck, I developed a list of people I wanted to speak with and sent out letters. I made sure to mention the reason I wanted to meet and why I believed that they would be able to make valuable contributions to my research. I followed up on the letters with a phone call. (Interviews with high-level officials needed to be arranged at least several weeks in advance, but it was easier to get most staff members to commit to a meeting if I called no more than two weeks ahead of my visit. The shorter time frame meant that they had a better sense of their schedules and availability. Some people even asked that I call to set up a meeting after arriving in town.)

While persistence usually paid off, there were some people I was never able to see. On the surface, this was a matter of scheduling—I lived in another city and carried out my research during a series of visits to Washington, D.C. In reality, however, scheduling difficulties often masked a basic unwillingness to be interviewed. In retrospect, I realize that the meetings with these few individuals, if they had occurred, would not have been very enlightening. Reluctance to meet almost certainly would have carried over into a reluctance to share important information.

Both of us conveyed to prospective interview subjects that we approached our research in an objective and unbiased manner. The World Bank has been taken by surprise in the past when seemingly sympathetic researchers have been granted access to the organization only to write scathing critiques once their research was completed. While these experiences have receded in time, they continue to exercise a restraining influence on the willingness of bank personnel to share information. It was essential to show that we had no axes to grind and that we needed and welcomed the organization's cooperation in drawing accurate conclusions about our topics.

Access Does Not Equal Information

In evaluating our ability to gain access, the first question was whether we were able to carry out the interviews needed for our projects. By this measure, we were fairly successful, as most of the people we contacted agreed to meet with us. A second dimension of access is harder to quantify. It is not sufficient just to conduct the interview; we also needed to have our questions answered and get good-quality information from interview subjects. The results in this area were more mixed. Some interviewees, not surprisingly, knew more than others.

Equally important, some were more willing to share information. In part, the degree of openness depended on the level of the staff member. As a rule, the most senior managers tended to be the most reticent, usually presenting views that had already been made public. Junior staff, loath to overstep the bounds of bank privacy, could also be hesitant about sharing information. Many of the most valuable insights were offered by midlevel managers, high enough up the ladder to have a good view of what was happening and less concerned about their position within the organization than their more junior colleagues. The quality of our interviews also depended in some cases on where within the bank an individual worked. People who felt that their area lay somewhat outside the mainstream of bank activities could be very outspoken. Deeply committed to their agendas, they welcomed any opportunity to share information about it with an outsider.

One corollary of the World Bank's emphasis on privacy is that it is extremely unusual for a researcher to tape record his or her interviews. While we would have liked to record our interviews, we understood that this was out of the question. Some staff members become anxious just seeing a researcher take out a notepad, and we needed to assure all of our interview subjects that the notes we were taking were for our own purposes only.

These are some of the guidelines we arrived at for ensuring that access translated into information:

- It was important to be well prepared, to have read the writings of the interviewee and have a good understanding of how the bank was going about its work in a given area.
- It was important to speak the technical language of the bank and to understand how economists approached the questions we were asking.
- Questions were prepared in advance, but being flexible allowed the interviewee to talk about related issues that we might not have thought of.
- It was important to remain alert to signs of hidden agendas in interpreting the response to questions.
- It helped to be sensitive to different subcultures within the organization and express an affinity for the background and experience of the person being interviewed.
- It is good practice to keep one's own attitudes out of the picture, while conveying as high a degree of knowledge and expertise about the organization as possible. World Bank staff members almost always find themselves with too many claims on their time. They are unwilling to spend the effort to educate a novice in the basics of their operations (knowledge that can be gained from published sources), but they will

respond well to someone who has done his or her homework and arrives at an interview with focused questions and a clear agenda.

- In terms of presentation, we both presented ourselves as professionals, dressing in business clothing and making clear that we had a certain status and level of knowledge based on our previous work experience.

Even with careful preparation and good interview skills, it is possible to gain access yet obtain relatively little useful information. A common problem is the inability to get staff and managers to depart from or go beyond the "party line." For example, the World Bank engages in more public self-confession than most organizations through published project evaluations, audits, and management speeches. It can be difficult, however, to get people to talk about the substance behind these findings. Instead of a deeper analysis, what one often hears is a parroting of the findings of the evaluation report.

One way to supplement the information provided by the bank and to understand better the context in which it is offered is to speak with people outside the organization. This might include former employees or consultants or people working at government agencies, news organizations, or nongovernmental organizations. In general, outsiders or former employees are more willing to speak frankly about the World Bank than those currently working there. From outside sources, we were able to learn a great deal about the bank's internal politics—a topic that staff members often avoid. However, in evaluating the information provided by these sources, one must remain aware of their personal agendas and their new organizations' stances toward the bank.

Exiting but Staying Connected

In concluding our interviews, we kept open avenues for future contact, as we needed to be able to check facts, get approval for quotations, and ask follow-up questions. We relied on e-mail or the telephone to stay in touch. There are important benefits to keeping the lines of communication open. Often, subjects are more forthcoming in a second or third conversation than they are in an initial meeting. Also, valuable assistance can be obtained by asking those interviewed whether they would be willing to read a draft of what the researcher is writing. Not only can readers correct mistaken impressions or conclusions, but the researcher may enter into an ongoing dialogue that can help clarify his or her thinking and improve the quality of the finished product. When a book or manuscript is ultimately completed, another round of thanks and perhaps a complimentary copy for those who were particularly helpful can cement this relationship and stimulate interest in the research within the institution.

Help from Unexpected Places:
Access and Assistance from within an Organization

Amy Wrzesniewski, Jane E. Dutton, and Gelaye Debebe

Three Women and a Cleaning Study

Our section describes how we found our way into a professional medical setting to interview cleaning staff about how their interactions with others in the workplace influenced their experience of the job and feelings about the work,[14] how they did their work,[15] and how they crafted the tasks and relationships in the job.[16] The study participants were a random sample of twenty-nine cleaning staff of a large university hospital. Our project team consisted of three people affiliated with the same university as the hospital: a white female business school professor of organizational behavior, a senior female Ph.D. student in organizational behavior from Ethiopia, and a senior white female Ph.D. student in psychology. We were all new to this topic, although one of us had negotiated research access in hospitals. Our common identity through the university may have eased our access.

Luck with Weak Ties

Access to the setting was indirect and was achieved through an incremental, bottom-up process. The lead author, Amy, managed the access process by building on indirect connections from working with a different faculty member who had hospital contacts with middle management. Our contact suggested that we contact a manager of supervisors in the cleaning department. It is this person (we will call her Grace) who arranged our access and helped us at every turn. Our story of attaining research access centers on the good fortune of meeting Grace.

Grace managed supervisors in the department of hospital cleaners. Initially, we phoned Grace, explained who we were, how we had found her, and what we were hoping to achieve. She invited us to send a research proposal. We composed one, describing our research purpose, our data needs, and timetable. From that point forward, we conversed with Grace mostly over e-mail. For approximately a year and half, Grace managed our access, as we moved from focus groups to exploratory interviews, and, finally, to the core interviews. As the study evolved, we gave Grace our "wish lists" (e.g., interviewing hospital cleaners from all shifts and units). Each time, she would respond positively, suggesting many ways to ease our next step. Grace would often do complex coordination and scheduling work to make the next project phase happen.

Being in Good Graces

It is an understatement to say that our project would not have happened without Grace. Access to the hospital cleaners was difficult, and so we relied on Grace and her communication with unit supervisors. We were in a vulnerable position; without someone inside the organization willing to champion our cause, it was unlikely that people would have agreed to be interviewed.

To our surprise, Grace volunteered to take this function on as her responsibility. We were willing to stuff mailboxes, schedule interviews, and manage the entire process. Grace seemed to foresee the difficulties we would have as outsiders navigating the system. The cleaners were hard to reach at work, relying on beepers for contact. As well, staff changed with each shift, and unit assignments changed daily in response to other cleaners' absences.

Grace volunteered to contact all interviewees, describe the study, schedule interview times, and find replacement interviewees, if necessary. As well, she helped us shape a realistic timetable, using her knowledge of how quickly information flowed in her unit and how easily interviews could be arranged. This work was not part of her job, but she treated it as if it were.

Grace's cooperation exceeded our expectations, and while we attribute much of it to her kindness, we also worked hard to create a positive connection. From the start, we communicated what we needed and shared all relevant information with her. As well, we acknowledged the help she offered after each exchange through e-mail or a phone call. By actively attending to our relationship with Grace, we avoided many pitfalls and the potential for lost momentum.

The Mechanics: Schedules, Rooms, and Time Off

The interview portion of the study was challenging. Cleaners' supervisors were asked to apprise interviewees of our study and let them know when, where, and for how long they were scheduled to meet with us. Because we did not have direct contact with supervisors, we relied on Grace to play the key linking role. Unfortunately, supervisors did not always relay information to interviewees, and we often had to reschedule interviews. Grace came to our rescue, putting us in touch with the cleaners' dispatch office, where we could beep cleaners to ask whether we could conduct the interview at the appointed time. In her efforts to help, she even offered to "leave nasty notes" for the supervisors she managed, in an attempt to increase response to our project.

We conducted interviews in the cleaners' break room or in an empty office in the dispatch suite. Grace established a contact person in the dispatch office for us; Betsy provided invaluable help with interview logistics. We often arrived at the hospital to find that an interviewee had not shown. Betsy would patiently contact the supervisors of each no-show, clarify the issue, and reschedule our interviews. Like Grace, she treated this work as part of her job.

Developing Rapport

We developed relationships on three fronts: with Grace, with the cleaners, and with Betsy and the dispatch office. Our relationship with Grace eased rapport with the cleaners and facilitated learning hospital terminology. Our first challenge was learning about the cleaning jobs. Many of the unit names and job descriptions were difficult. Sensing our confusion, Grace connected us to Camille, an especially helpful supervisor. Camille described each unit and the meaning of the cryptic job titles assigned to categories of cleaners. Armed with this knowledge, we were able to make informed decisions about sample selection. However, we soon learned that the job tasks and materials had their own mysterious names. We asked cleaners to explain the terms to us, which facilitated our asking far more informed questions. By the end of the project, we could ask questions about "encountering sharps," "pulling trash," and "doing a discharge."

To develop rapport with the cleaners, we gave them full explanations of the study, tried to make them feel comfortable about being audiotaped, and made clear that they could skip questions or stop the interview at any time. This became easier as the interviews progressed, and word that the interviews were enjoyable traveled between coworkers. We tried to show our respect and appreciation for the cleaner's knowledge and time. We saw our role as that of learners, asking cleaners to describe their work and posing thoughtful follow-up questions.

In weekly research meetings, we reflected on our interview experiences. Although we did not collect data on how race and ethnicity may have affected rapport, we did discuss the subtle and complex dynamics taking place in our interactions with the cleaners, dynamics that evolved around our racial identities. Specifically, the Ethiopian member of the research team had an experience that was repeated in several interviews with African-American cleaners. She described "a look" cleaners would give her, followed by an awkwardness in the flow of the conversation. This look often occurred when she asked for cleaners' insights about why things happened in particular ways in their interactions with others in the hospital. Having lived in the United States for over seventeen years, she had come to interpret this look as a nonverbal sign that she violated the assumption of a shared racial experience. Although she did not discuss what this look meant or why the conversation was awkward with the cleaner, she wondered about the meaning of the look. Was it meant to convey the message, "How come *you're* asking what should be an obvious thing to you as a black person?" She handled the breaks in conversation followed by this look by showing sincere interest and exploring the issues raised in greater depth. She hoped her verbal and nonverbal responses would convey the message, "I'm not pretending I don't understand, but I cannot assume anything. I need to know, in your own words." In many cases, she felt her response was met with a dissolving of the awkwardness and a resumption of the dialogue.

When we reflected on this experience as a group, we found an interesting contrast in the experiences of the white members of the research team. Instead of expecting that the interviewer would "understand" racial dynamics, several of the African-American cleaners explained, unsolicited, the race attributions associated with particular incidents and stories. These explanations were meant to clarify the subtleties in the cleaners' interactions that they attributed to race or ethnicity. Beyond these extra explanations offered to the white interviewers, we detected no other obvious differences in our experiences with the cleaners.

Finally, we were often aware of the possibility that our presence could be an imposition for the dispatch office. For instance, the empty office that was made available to us was actually used by staff to make telephone calls, store supplies, and hang coats. During our interviews, none of the dispatch office staff interrupted us to use the room. While we did not develop a relationship with the staff, we were not made to feel as if we were in their way.

A Graceful Exit?

We made a small attempt to show appreciation by giving cleaners business school coffee mugs. We also sent interview transcripts to their homes, providing an opportunity to correct it or drop out of the study. We also sent our research report to those who requested it.

While we tried to create a reciprocal relationship with the cleaners, we later felt that we had not done enough to give back to them. In several interviews, cleaners shared powerful emotions, personal stories, and often painful experiences of doing this work. On more than one occasion, cleaners cried when recounting negative work experiences. It felt awkward to offer only a coffee cup and a promise of the transcript and a research report at the end of such a powerful exchange. Some of the cleaners asked us whether we planned to help them by sharing what we had learned about the devaluation of their work with the hospital administration. We could only respond that we were trying to learn more about their occupation to communicate the experience of doing this work to a broader audience. We had made no plans to take action in the hospital after conducting these interviews, and we had to admit that to the cleaners who wanted us to use our position of relative power to effect change.

We felt much better about the way we managed our exit with Grace, Betsy, and the others who helped us. At the conclusion of the interviews, we surprised

Grace, bringing her a gift and a thank you from each of us. In keeping with her character, Grace protested that it was unnecessary. A plan to take Grace out for lunch was canceled when we learned how busy she was; it would be asking even more of her to take time out for us. We surprised Betsy and the other employees in the dispatch office by bringing flowers to thank them. We left the hospital in such a way that we felt we could return and be welcomed to do further research.

Future Promises to Ourselves: Lessons Learned

We have learned many lessons through this project. Some lessons concern things we would do differently next time, while others concern things we would surely do again. We negotiated informal access to the hospital; the project evolved over time and allowed us great flexibility. However, this kind of "sideways" access meant that we had no formal arrangements for giving back in a more meaningful way to study participants. We felt a lack of closure and a sense of unease about this lost opportunity to share our findings with participants and to hear their responses. In the future, we plan to create balanced exchanges with participants, through avenues such as payment and sharing findings in workshops.

We learned a delightful lesson in doing research in an organization that was "right in our backyard." Often, researchers conduct studies in organizations with which they have no affiliation. We found it very satisfying to do our project in a hospital with which we were affiliated, as it eased research in two ways. First, the short distance between our offices and the organization minimized difficulties. Second, we established trust and rapport more quickly because of our common insider status. We were given great latitude, much cooperation, and extra help.

The informality of our arrangement was a double-edged sword. While it provided latitude and allowed changes as the research evolved, it also introduced coordination difficulties. All of the setup work happened behind the scenes, giving us no control over the process. While Grace did a magnificent job of making the interviews happen, we were frustrated at our inability to speak directly with the supervisors and cleaners. On the other hand, the informality gave us the chance to work closely with Grace, which was deeply satisfying. It is possible that Grace took the role she did to limit the relationship we had with supervisors and cleaners, allowing her to control the terms of the project in ways that helped all involved.

In closing, we realize that the loose form of permission granted was likely related to the type of job we studied. Had we studied a higher-status job, higher barriers to gaining research approval may have been in place. We will never know, but we suspect that this is the case.

Notes

1. See, for example, Malcolm Spector, "Learning to Study Public Figures," in *Fieldwork Experience, Qualitative Approaches to Social Research*, ed. William B. Shaffier, Robert A. Stebbins, and Allan Turowetz (New York: St. Martin's, 1980); Sally Engle Merry, *Getting Justice and Getting Even* (Chicago: University of Chicago Press, 1990); and Kristin Luker, *Abortion and the Politics of Motherhood* (Berkeley: University of California Press, 1984).

2. Spector, "Learning to Study Public Figures," 101.

3. Charles M. Judd, Eliot R. Smith, and Louise H. Kidder, *Research Methods in Social Relations* (London: Holt, Rinehart & Winston, 1991), 218.

4. See, for example, Spector, "Learning to Study Public Figures," 102.

5. Spector, "Learning to Study Public Figures," 101.

6. Spector, "Learning to Study Public Figures."

7. H. W. Perry, *Deciding to Decide: Agenda Setting in the United States Supreme Court* (Cambridge, Mass.: Harvard University Press, 1991), 10.

8. Hoffman, "Problems of Access," 46.

9. Hoffman, "Problems of Access," 47.

10. Stoller, *The Taste of Ethnographic Things*.

11. Publications resulting from this research include Ted G. Jelen, *The Political Mobilization of Religious Beliefs* (New York: Praeger, 1991); Ted G. Jelen, "Politicized Group Identification: The Case of Fundamentalism," *Western Political Quarterly* 44 (1991): 33–52; Ted G. Jelen, "Political Christianity: A Contextual Analysis," *American Journal of Political Science* 36 (August 1992): 692–714; Ted G. Jelen, "The Clergy and Abortion," *Review of Religious Research* 34 (1992): 132–51; Ted G. Jelen, "The Political Consequences of Religious Group Attitudes," *Journal of Politics* 55 (February 1993): 178–90; Ted G. Jelen, *The Political World of the Clergy* (New York: Praeger, 1993); Ted G. Jelen, "Protestant Clergy as Political Leaders: Theological Limitations," *Review of Religious Research* 36 (1994): 23–42.

12. See Michelle Miller-Adams, *The World Bank: New Agendas in a Changing World* (London: Routledge, 1999).

13. This research will appear in Charles T. Meyers, "Teaching States How to Govern: The World Bank and Governance in the 1990s," Ph.D. diss., University of Michigan, forthcoming.

14. Jane E. Dutton, Galaye Debebe, and Amy Wrzesniewski, "Being Valued and Devalued at Work: A Social Valuing Perspective on Relationship Sensemaking," unpublished manuscript, 1999.

15. Galaye Debebe and Jane E. Dutton, "Getting through the Day: The Use of Relational Knowledge in Everyday Task Execution," unpublished manuscript, 1999.

16. Amy Wrzesniewski and Jane E. Dutton, "Crafting a Job: Revisioning Employees as Active Crafters of Their Work," *Academy of Management Review* 26, no. 2 (2001): 179–201.

Gaining Access for Interviewing and Observation

8

SOMETIMES A RESEARCHER may want to gain access for a project that will require interviewing but also involves observation over a longer period of time. As the stories in this chapter demonstrate, there are varying degrees of interviewing and observation. The researchers presented here negotiated access to individuals who were part of a range of organizations, including state bureaucratic organizations (public welfare offices), human service organizations that have characteristics of a quasi-governmental system, and formal state institutions (prisons).

As in other chapters, these researchers sought different levels of access. Lin's study was primarily based on interviewing, though observation provided important validation. She spent three weeks, ten to twelve hours per day, in each prison she studied and asked for the freedom to roam freely. This approach allowed her to "balance the interview data with my own observations of events in the prison."[1] By contrast, Daniel-Echols's and Sandfort's studies relied at least as much on the researcher's observations as on the interviews.

For the researchers whose stories are presented in this chapter, interviewing generally preceded and provided an entrée to the more in-depth and sometimes more intrusive, observational part of their study. Conducting this kind of research often requires a researcher to think carefully about the people he or she might want to observe as well as the role the researcher will play in the everyday lives of people in that environment. Observers generally spend more time in the site than those only conducting interviews and thus must contemplate the relationship they will have with those in the site. For example, the time spent in the site may lead informants to become friendly with and otherwise interact with the researcher, forcing the researcher to respond in ways appropriate to a relationship that is neither friendship nor that of a stranger.

From a relational standpoint, observing raises issue two important issues. The first of these is whether the researchers are engaged in socially acceptable behavior. Observers must straddle the line between being visible and invisible. Observational research thus places researchers in an uncomfortable position, as they watch and record others' interaction without comment. While everyone else in the site is reacting to an event, the observer, as a person who is supposed to be invisible, is barred from showing emotion. The vignettes in this chapter also raise an increasingly complicated picture of the role of identity in the access process. Identity is a core matter, but the aspects of identity that a researcher may think are important are often less salient than other unanticipated aspects of identity that come to the forefront.

The Challenges of "Hanging Around"

In Richard Fenno's groundbreaking study of the U.S. House of Representatives, he secured access to legislators in two different sites—on Capitol Hill and in their home districts. He observed representatives in their home districts as they responded to a variety of constituents and their concerns. His catchall phrase—"hanging around"—captures the dynamics of this aspect of observational research: "When I am with each House member, I do a lot of what I call in the Introduction 'hanging around.' That is, a lot of watching, listening, and talking, a lot of sitting, standing and riding, some participation and a lot of questioning—all for the purpose of collecting data."[2]

Though observation may seem easy—just watching, questioning, and listening—researchers' access accounts suggest that the process of observation often brings with it unexpected interpersonal challenges. In this longer quote, Fenno quite pointedly chronicles the solitary feelings and lack of attention that develop for researchers as they pursue this highly nebulous activity of hanging around:

> Despite the frenzy of activity all around, the role of the observer is very solitary. You are marginal—deliberately so—to every group you are with. Rarely will anyone come up to make you feel at home—at a dinner, a cocktail party, a celebration, a meeting. They are playing their games. The House member is playing with them. The more the member is interacting person to person with others, the less can the participant observer either participate or observe. . . . Although no one in this gathering of total strangers is paying the slightest attention to you, you can give no indication of being anything less than completely comfortable, of not thoroughly enjoying yourself. . . . It is a lonesome duty; and anyone who tends toward paranoia should not volunteer.[3]

Researchers battle not just loneliness but possibly also anxiety in their role as observers. Relative to other forms of research, like interviewing, for instance, in observational research the boundaries between researcher and informant are much less clearly defined. For instance, in one of the stories in this section, Sandfort, who was able to utilize preexisting protocols of the public welfare offices that allow trainees to "shadow" more experienced workers, highlights the feelings of anxiety that arose in making everyday decisions while in the midst of her observational research. While her behavior would have felt normal had she actually *been* a trainee, as a researcher it did not. She describes feeling as if she was "walking on eggshells" because she could not easily adapt to such an undefined interpersonal role. Fenno similarly describes this type of research as demanding physical and emotional work.[4]

From a relational standpoint, the ideas of hanging around and various forms of participant observation seem to break with the defining characteristics of ordinary relationships: reciprocity and role definition. There are not any ordinary relationships that mirror or contain the characteristics of shadowing and other kinds of observational research. Two quasi-relationships that are somewhat similar to observational research are that of a voyeur and a stalker. Both of those types of quasi-relationships are extreme and tend to be outside the boundary of acceptable forms of social interaction over long periods of time.[5]

Being Present and Not Participating

Part of the challenge in observational research that researchers wrestle with is one of being present and yet not participating. If reciprocity is a main element in most relationships, in observational work this experience is often missing. A researcher is often privy to a range of emotional situations that he or she observes but can say or do nothing about. Through various types of observational research, researchers may share intimate physical space and time with another person(s) and yet not interact with them in a significant way that would lead to the establishment of trust or the development of rapport.

As Fenno notes earlier, observation research can also put a researcher in strained interpersonal situations with others with whom informants come into contact—individuals who are not being directly observed—in a particular research environment. Being placed in these types of situations heightens the researcher's attention to his or her own conduct. As a person who is not supposed to draw attention to him or herself, the researcher may be especially reluctant to behave in a way that might catch the attention of outsiders and provoke the need to explain one's presence in the site. As Fenno suggests, a researcher in observational research is always judging "the situation for its appropriateness, its ripeness."[6] These issues have even more salience for more extended periods of observation and will be addressed in the next chapter as well.

The Role of Identity

Part of the difficulty that identity presents in the access process is that it may take time to discern where one fits into an organization one wants to observe. Sandfort and Daniel-Echols relied on signals provided by the organizations they studied. Interestingly enough, Lin was able to construct an identity as someone who was not scared, threatened, or intimidated in the midst of a prison. She talked to prisoners "face-to-face, with no bars or screens, in rooms with the door closed." This also helped her develop trust among both staff and prisoners.

Daniel-Echols's multiple identities allowed both staff and clients to classify her as an insider at different points in the research. As someone who often looked like the clients that the agency she was studying was trying to help, she gained firsthand experience about how they were served. Being identified as an insider was not always attractive to Daniel-Echols. When she tried to create distance and identify herself as an outsider, however, she was not able to. Her identity as an African American mother still identified her as part of an insider group.

Exit

The more embedded the researcher is in the context, with the informant, the harder it becomes to leave the environment. Issues of how one disengages from the site begin to become an issue. Observation requires that researchers spend more time in the environment; consequently, the researchers in this chapter often became more embedded in the environments they were researching. This sustained engagement may lead to the development of rapport with individuals and to a deeper connection with one's informants. For the contributors who engaged in observation (chapters 8–10), the deeper connection with informants made it hard to walk away, and it influenced the write-up of the research even after they left the site.

Going to Prison

Ann Chih Lin

In March 1992, I stepped off a plane in a state I had never visited and made my shaky way down miles of country roads to a prison I call Antelope Valley. It was the first of my visits to five male, medium-security prisons for a study of prison rehabilitation. The book from that research is based on 354 open-ended interviews with staff and prisoners and on observations from prison classrooms and workshops, at staff meetings, and on the grounds.[7] The number and range of prisons—four federal and one state—made it the largest multi-site qualitative study of prisons in the United States.

As a graduate student, I was completely unaware of how difficult this would be—a good thing, too, because if I had been, the project would never have gotten done. Getting access to the prisons was a collaborative effort. Many people opened doors, vouched for me, or took a chance on trusting me. In return, I worked to be worthy of their trust. The process taught me that researchers often have little to give those they study. Often, we can only accept, with gratitude and grace.

Asking Early

My introduction to access was as blissful as it could possibly have been. One of the country's experts on prisons was at my university, in another department. Though I had never taken a course with him, he agreed to introduce me to both the Federal Bureau of Prisons (BOP) and to a state prison system. I also called a second expert, at a different university, on the advice of a professor whom I knew. He not only gave me his time but promised—and delivered—letters of recommendation to top administrators in the BOP.

Apart from the fact that I was studying in a strong graduate department, neither of these men had any reason to go out of their way for me. My early ideas were rough and often ignorant, which they must have known. But I realize now that my enthusiasm and willingness to incorporate their suggestions probably made them feel like they were not wasting their efforts. Had I approached them later, with hypotheses that I was unwilling to change, it would have been harder to obtain—and accept!—their help.

From this I learned: Ask for help, even from people who have no apparent reason to help you, and ask early. Many people I telephoned ignored me. But had I not attempted to contact a number of well-known people, I would never have had the chance to work with any of them. And since I was asking early, the people who did help later felt invested in me. Particularly in a field such as prison research, where everyone knows everyone else, this sponsorship was invaluable. Without it, my work would never have gotten off the ground.

Using Influence

Getting permission to do research at the BOP is a lengthy process, requiring approval from the Office of Research and Evaluation, advisory groups representing correctional workers and prisoners, the warden of every prison one wishes to enter, and the regional directors. Luckily, the staff in the Office of Research and Evaluation became both my teachers and my advocates. We spent a long time crafting a proposal that went through the details: proposing that I be given a body alarm, asking to locate most of my work in a specified area, providing that all interviews were to take place only when the prison schedule allowed. Then the research put their own credibility on the line, persuading their on-site staff at one prison to take responsibility for me. Nine months after I had defended my proposal and five months after I had formally applied to do research in the BOP, I finally got into my first prison.

Yet even after that visit passed smoothly, other wardens were still dubious. A naturally risk-averse breed, the wardens were sure I would disrupt the normal operations of the prison. I was asking for a particularly long stay (ten to twelve hours each day for three weeks); for interviews that might interfere with the normal routine; and for freedom of movement within the prison compound. While unwilling to refuse the research staff outright, they simply ignored my inquiries.

At that point, the prison expert at my university invited me to dinner with Michael Quinlan, then the director of the BOP. Quinlan was intrigued to hear that I had visited one of his prisons and kindly invited me to return. Not one to pass up an opportunity, I mentioned that I had asked to go to several other prisons but that the wardens were worried that I would pose a security risk.

"Oh, that's certainly appropriate," he said, "but I'm sure you wouldn't present a problem."

Within two weeks, I had permission to go to the other federal prisons.

Does this story suggest that access is simply a matter of knowing the right people? Certainly without my adviser's intervention, the project would have been in jeopardy. But the groundwork I had laid made it possible for him to use his influence. Because I had a carefully crafted proposal and some experience when my adviser talked to Director Quinlan, I was less of a gamble. While Quinlan could not be sure that I would not antagonize prisoners, play havoc with security regulations, or put myself in a compromising position, he had some evidence of my reliability. The same is true with the influence exerted by the research staff: Because they spent time working with me, they were more confident that their colleagues in the prison could work with me as well.

The use of influence raises another issue. Was my research compromised by the fact that wardens felt pressure to let me in? Given Director Quinlan's intervention, I worried that wardens might think I was a spy for the administration. But the problem was not as severe as I expected. So much time elapsed between getting permission to do my research and actually arriving at the prison that the wardens barely remembered who I was, much less why they had approved my visit in the first place. I also found that the word of my advisers, the researchers from the Office of Research and Evaluation, and even of Director Quinlan mattered very little when it came to the individual prisoner or correctional staffer. As the next section shows, I had to transform my formal access into consent on the ground.

Building Confidence

Two weeks into one of my prisons, I was taking notes at a prisonwide staff meeting when I suddenly heard the warden say my name. "Some of you may have met Ann Lin, a researcher who's been here to learn about us the last couple of weeks. Unlike most visitors, we hardly know she's here, and we're pretty happy about that!"

Unlikely though it sounds, this comment was actually a compliment. Prison staff often tell of visitors who arrive, disrupt everyone's routine, and pontificate, whether or not they've "spent time in the trenches." So I tried to listen and observe unobtrusively and made an effort not to interfere with prison routines or to criticize anyone (staff or prisoners) openly. For instance, when I interviewed staff, I adjusted my plans to theirs. I climbed up a watchtower to interview one officer and interviewed others standing on guard. If a staff member had to speak to a prisoner, run an errand, or answer the phone, I stopped the interview. If we had to do part of the interview one day and finish on another, I agreed. If an appointment, or several, were cancelled, I never got upset. Such actions did more than words to make me easy to be around.

Another way in which visitors can be disruptive is to be scared. Visitors who seem uncomfortable make both staff and prisoners conscious that prisons (and, by implication, they themselves) are abnormal and that their lives are on display. So I did my best to behave as if I were in any other group of people. For instance, I insisted on interviewing in private, unmonitored settings. This meant that I talked to prisoners the way that staff did: face to face, with no bars or screens, in rooms with the door closed. While this was a safety risk, it was the same risk that staff—and prisoners—ran daily. My willingness to run this risk showed that I trusted the people whom I was asking to trust me.

It is important to be clear, however, that while I could try not to be a nuisance, normalizing my presence was impossible. By definition, interviewing and observing staff and prisoners meant that people's lives *were* on display. Therefore, I had to establish that I would be impartial, treating everybody and their information with respect.

To do this, I relied on three things that cannot be taken for granted in a prison: explanations, courtesy, and humanity. Before each interview, I would shake the person's hand, explain who I was, answer questions, and give him the chance to refuse to speak. I treated anyone who refused the interview with courtesy. I gave prisoners and staff the same description of who I was, so that neither group would feel that I was lying. I introduced myself to as many people as possible, whether or not they were on my random list of interview subjects, and did not spend too much time with any one person, lest I be accused of favoritism.

News travels fast in a prison, and I knew that any disrespect or arrogance on my part would have long-range repercussions. But the staff and prisoners, with very few exceptions, treated me with politeness, friendliness, and warmth. The moral of the story is one that I heard often in prison: "If you treat a man human, he'll treat you human." The staff and prisoners treated me human, and I tried to do the same.

Looking Back

Working from a graduate student budget, I could do few of the things that researchers can do to repay those that have helped them. I had no money to compensate my respondents; I contributed no training, no equipment, and no information. I made the classic mistake of the novice researcher, promising people copies of the book when it appeared—a promise that took eight years to redeem. Ten years after my first visit, I am still only beginning to learn how to make my work directly useful to practitioners.

With more experience and more money, I could have designed a study that would have been more immediately helpful to the prisons or that at least made a point of producing nonacademic updates on my work. As it was, however, it was pretty obvious to everyone that they were doing me a favor and that little if any of the research would ever come back to them.

Research is sometimes—often—like this. Our sense that we will have something to give back can be born as much out of arrogance as from gratitude. Good academic research—even good policy research—will often not meet the immediate needs of those we study. It may not even arouse their interest. This does not mean that we should not try to do both of these things. But it does mean that we should not count on it for access. Instead, depending on the goodwill of others, and acting so as to deserve it, will always play a part in making our way into a research site.

How I Got Them to Talk to Me: The Importance of Persistence, Personality, and Identity

Marijata Daniel-Echols

For my investigation of the impact of politics on the day-to-day implementation of welfare-to-work programs, I was able to gain access to three organizations running such programs in Detroit. Two of the organizations were profit agencies, and the third was a nonprofit organization. Within each program I conducted participant observations as well as one-on-one, semistructured interviews with program staff members and clients.[8]

Preparing to Enter the Field and Developing a Hook

I had initially conceived of my fieldwork, from access to exit, as a process that I would be able to plan and control. With that mind-set, my strategy for identifying and gaining access to potential sites was very logical. To develop my list of possible cases, I used my previous experience as a summer intern at a Detroit foundation (during which I had visited some organizations and learned which government agencies managed aspects of the welfare-to-work program and which organizations had established reputations in the city) and the knowledge of other university students and faculty who had done or were doing related projects.

I developed what I thought was a straightforward pitch as my hook. I first sent potential sites a letter on university letterhead introducing my project and myself. In that letter, I briefly explained who I was and my connection to another university research project with which the organization was familiar. I stated what I wanted from the organization and the amount of time I anticipated that I needed to get that information. The letter included a date on which I planned to call to follow up the letter with a discussion.

The Need for Persistence

As I prepared and mailed my letters, I started to realize that my expectation to plan and control all aspects of the process of gaining access was naïve. For example, it took weeks of voice-mail limbo and an in-person visit to get a comprehensive list of current welfare-to-work provider agencies. Once I received that list, I sent letters to the people identified by the administering city agency as each organization's contact person. Often the information the city had given me was out of date, so that some letters were sent to incorrect addresses or the wrong person. These types of uncontrollable factors delayed my efforts to gain access.

It took me two months of writing letters and calling to gain access to my first site. When I exited that first site, I was able to use that experience as a reference and a source of credibility when approaching new organizations. Even so, it took two months after leaving the first case to find a second. Since I had a good relationship with the director of my first case, I went to her and asked for names of possible people to contact for a third case. This tactic did gain me entry to a third organization, but it still took another two months of calls and letters between the second and third cases. In the interim I was rejected by several organizations.

The reasons why I was rejected varied. Some organizations were distrustful of outside researchers. One program director told me quite directly that "nobody cares about client outcomes" and that I should find a more important dissertation topic. The contractual relationship between Detroit and the implementing organizations also meant that there existed potential political pitfalls. For example, one

organization in particular worried that simply by having me on the site and talking to their clients I would endanger their contract with the city, despite my explanations that I had no government affiliation and that I was bound by university
rules of research ethics.

In the end, I solicited eight organizations to find three that would allow me
access. I found that I had to be willing to broaden what I believed to be acceptable as cases. Some of the organizations I approached were places that I had felt I
would settle for only if desperate. Some of them, including one that ended up being one of my three cases, I really didn't have much information about, but it
looked reasonable on paper. I also had to adjust my sales pitch. For example, my
first letters were too academic and too long, because I thought I had to prove that
I knew what I was talking about to establish credibility. Ultimately, I ended up
with three short paragraphs. I also continuously tweaked my phone pitches from
call to call based on how they were received or rejected.

Getting My Foot in the Door
and the Influence of Personality

When I was able to get face-to-face interviews based on my letter and phone calls,
the meetings turned out to be the organization director's chance to give me a once-
over. Had I not connected personally with each of them at that first meeting, I
might not have had the success in gathering data within their programs. I know
this to be the case at one organization where I was granted access only to have it
withdrawn two weeks into data collection. In that instance, I had my first meeting
not with the program director but with her second in command. While I got along
with the second in command, the director was leery of me as an outsider. She was
protective of her program and worried that she didn't "know anything about
[me]" personally. After a few tension-filled days at the site, she informed me that
I could no longer observe her program or talk to her clients. At another site, I had
several staff members respond to my request for an interview with "as long as my
boss knows and says its OK"; I could assure them that their boss did know and
that it was OK to talk with me.

Identity and Credibility

I am convinced that my ability to gain the trust of organization staff members and
clients was based partly on personality but a great deal more on identity. In my case,
being a young black woman and mother worked to my advantage on both meaningful and superficial levels. Superficially, I looked like all the other clients sitting
in the program. This allowed me to observe without being flagged as an outsider
unless I chose to identify myself. I also was able to enter into casual conversations

with clients about the program. Many times clients would ask me questions, thinking that I also was a client who might have information about particular case workers or the program. Being mistaken for a client allowed me to see how clients were treated. I had several experiences in which a staff person either did not recognize me or had not yet been introduced to me. In those situations, I was treated with less of their attention and willingness to help me than when they found out I was a researcher. I went from being "Hon" to "Ms. Echols." I moved from being another face in the room to someone to be catered to.

This type of blending in at times seemed a bit too close to deception for my comfort. However, I found that after identifying myself as an outsider to staff and clients, my race, gender, age, and motherhood status caused individuals within the organization still to identify me as part of their group. I had several staff members (all black women) at one site tell me that they were proud of me as a black woman getting her doctorate. I had conversations with clients about our children. During part of my fieldwork, I was pregnant with my second child. During that time I shared pregnancy tales with other expecting clients in the program. Some of the staff had a race consciousness that shaped their political views and the way they did their jobs. With those individuals being black and being interested in politics easily led to candid conversations on both topics.

Gaining access to individual staff members and clients went beyond initial identifications based on race and gender, age, and familial status. I still had to gain credibility for people to trust me enough to talk with me one on one and often on tape. I found that one of the best ways to gain this credibility was to demonstrate a true commitment to the project. I showed up when I said I would, on time, and consistently. I was there when it was ninety degrees with 90 percent humidity and no air conditioning. I was there when a rat had died in the heat duct and the whole place smelled like garbage. I was there when the hallways were flooded due to a water-main break. I was on the site for meetings that staff said would be boring and that I might want to skip. If a staff member mentioned a meeting or off-site event that they thought would be helpful to me, I went to that event with the staff person.

By simply being present, I gained credibility as someone who was serious about her work and wanted to learn. For clients this was particularly important. As a group they felt that their opinions were not taken into consideration. So for me to be willing to spend time voluntarily in a program that they were being forced to attend and then for me to ask them what they thought about the program impressed some clients.

An important issue of identity that I have not touched on yet is class. I quickly learned that my own class status was very different not just from clients (which I knew going into the project) but from staff as well. Many of the staff members I met were former clients. The suburbs were often used to represent a world distinct from their own and a world where everyone was "rich." I felt that divulging that I lived in a suburb would set me apart as an outsider to both staff and clients. Because

I had so many other identity similarities with the people I observed and interviewed, it was easy for me to start to discount our differences, to identify with them in ways that were not authentic. Comments made by staff members and clients that revealed their thoughts about class differences made me more aware of my status as an observer. It helped me balance between immersing myself in the environment and keeping an objective perspective.

Exiting the Field:
The Lasting Impact of Personality and Identity

I decided to leave each site when I thought that I had a good feel for the entirety of the program and had interviewed all of the staff members and as many clients as possible. I made a point of stressing to individual staff members and the program directors both in person and in writing that I was grateful for the help they had given me. I also told people that I would appreciate being able to come back and would ask questions to clarify my understanding when I was in the analysis phase of my work.

While my relationships with staff members and clients varied across the organizations in their warmth and depth, I left each case feeling an obligation to represent fairly the strengths, weaknesses, and intentions of staff members. Having connected along personality and identity lines with individuals, stepping away from the sites and analyzing my data strictly as an impartial observer was more difficult than I expected it to be. I did not want to betray the trust people had put in me by making critiques that seemed too scathing. I did not want my praise to appear indulgent to my academic readership. At the same time, there were some people I met while in the field for whom I had negative feelings. For example, I thought one staff member should be fired for performing poorly. In my writing, however, I had to balance my descriptions of his behavior with an analysis of how the organizational context enabled it. The process of gaining access and building rapport helped my analysis and writing as I described the unique features of each case and tried to make an argument that was accurate, honest, and fair.

Accessing Multiple Human Service Organizations
for Field-Based Research

Jodi Sandfort

In my work studying social policy implementation, the task of accessing the human service organizations is often formidable because of the need to approach multiple organizations within a social policy field. This essay draws on my experience in one of these projects—an in-depth study of organizations involved in the implementation of welfare reform.[9] This particular study was a comparative case study design that utilized ethnographic methods to understand front-line conditions better within these organizations.

In this study, my central research challenge was to understand and document the perspectives that workers develop through their daily work on the front lines of the welfare system; as a result, I taped semistructured interviews and focus groups, conducted extensive document reviews of organizational materials, and employed participant observation of day-to-day activities. I employed these methods in both public and private organizations, focusing on five agencies responsible for serving welfare recipients in two Michigan counties. Each type of organization had its own unique access context. The public welfare offices are part of a statewide bureaucratic organization that has formalized procedures for relationships with external researchers. In contrast, welfare-to-work agencies receive contracts from local administrative entities to provide services. These administrative organizations have neither authority nor formal processes to regulate the agencies' relationship with outside researchers.

In both settings, I relied on my ability to develop sincere relationships with professionals in the field to help me gain access to my research sites. In my conversations with state administrators, local managers, midline supervisors, and front-line workers, my identity as a young, white, midwestern woman with professional experience in human service organizations was an asset. In my experience, accessing human service organizations occurs through three stages. Although in practice these rarely occur linearly, they are recounted here as such for conceptual ease.

Learning about the Organizational Field

Researchers interested in organizationally based phenomena must invest in learning the context of the organization, what I will call here the "organizational field." In my area of social policy, that involves identifying the policy issues, professional norms, and administrative structure relevant to the topic of investigation. In the welfare study, I took considerable time learning about this before approaching individual organizations to participate. I held informational phone interviews with policymakers, local service providers, and policy advocates. I attended statewide human service conferences about welfare reform. I spent a day in a local public welfare office, observing staff meetings and interviewing managers. When talking with each informant, I would try to learn how he or she understood the policy area, the relevant actors, the important issues. These initial conversations were invaluable because they helped socialize me to the various perspectives and norms held by people occupying different positions in the field. They also allowed me to gather important internal memos and agency documents. Through each conversation, I built my legitimacy with players in the organizational field; over time, key state administrators were willing to provide me descriptive data and introductory letters that helped in the selection of and access to actual field sites.

In spite of these benefits, the interactions with professionals were not always easy. My affiliation with a large public university made me appear to some as being sheltered from the "real world." With new contacts, I often felt as if I was being tested by my informant. Was I someone worth taking the time to talk with? Had I done my homework so that I understood the relevant issues for local service providers? Did I know other people in the field who were respected? This process was challenging, because I needed to prove that I was informed, but also needed to learn more about the policy context. During this phase of learning about the organizational field, I reflected in my field notes:

> This process is so contrary to how we are taught to do research from textbooks or academic research. In this instance, my grounding in the academic literature would do me no good. In fact, I am having to make very specific choices about how I articulate this project [to these informants]. I can't frame my research questions from the perspective of the academic implications. Instead, I am putting myself in the shoes of those administrators within the system and thinking about what types of framing and questions would make sense to them. I do this instinctively. But it is certainly contrary to widely practiced academic or policy research methods.

I was learning that to access human service organizations, I had to establish real human connections with key professionals and convince them of my legitimacy in terms that they found relevant. I could not hide behind academic jargon or constructs.

Gaining Access to Particular Organizations

The second stage of accessing human service organizations is built on this foundation. Armed with data and contact names, I was better able to make informed decisions about the particular organizations relevant to my study design. In my experience, the authority to allow researchers to access a particular organization is held by the most senior manager, whether a local office director in a large public bureaucracy or the CEO of a nonprofit contractor, regardless of the formal research clearance process of the organization. I found that it was important to begin with an in-person meeting, where I could explain—in terms relevant to the manager—the nature of the investigation. This meeting allowed more opportunities to build rapport, dispel misimpressions, and clarify latent questions. I never used this time to hold a formal interview using my developed research protocols. Rather, I used the discussion as an opportunity to glean more information about the community, gather organizational charts, and identify key people who could assist once I was inside the organization.

This second stage of gaining access also can hold some challenges. The climate in some offices is charged; some social service organizations struggle with low staff morale and hostility to outsiders. Symptoms of such conditions are evident when researchers try to access the organization—phone calls might not be returned, or mid-level management might be nonresponsive in meetings. For researchers, such experiences can be disheartening and confusing, particularly when they contrast with the receptions given at other field sites. While my tendency was to overscrutinize my own actions—and search for something that I was doing differently—I came to realize that there were many factors in the internal organizational climate that are impossible to know from the outside. Overcoming these roadblocks required plain perseverance. When certain organizational gatekeepers were not available for initial meetings, I spoke to their assistants who could provide the necessary clearance. When some people didn't return my calls, I made repeated attempts.

Building Rapport with Individuals in Organizations

Once access to a particular organization is assured, researchers must progress to the final phase of accessing research subjects: identifying individual subjects. Drawing on the knowledge I gleaned in the first two phases of access, I developed techniques for conducting semistructured interviews and observation appropriate for the organizational context. In the public welfare offices where strong hierarchies existed, I accessed individuals for interviews by requesting supervisors to ask certain front-line workers for their consent. Because of the formalized structure in the local offices, I decided to observe daily practices, by "shadowing" different workers each day. I recruited subjects by approaching individuals at the end of one day, asking whether I could shadow them the following morning; while some refused, many felt that since I had been in the office, I must be harmless. With the smaller, private welfare-to-work contractors, where work is less structured, my strategies for access were different. In these organizations, I requested to be allowed to observe training classrooms and "talk" with staff. I approached certain workers once I was on-site for their consent to be interviewed. Initially, observation was carried out in the back of the classrooms. With the passage of time, however, I took on behaviors demonstrated by the workers themselves and moved between classroom and office, responding to various circumstances.

This third level of accessing human service organization also poses its own challenges. Soon after entering a new site, I wrote the following:

> It is hard at first when I go to a site to figure out how to fit in, how to position myself. Each day, I experience anxiety when I need to cultivate another worker to shadow or have to ask permission to stay an extra day. I often feel most uncomfortable around lunchtime—where should I eat, what shall I do during the time. . . . I always feel as if I am walking on eggshells.

With time, such emotions receded as I became more astute at navigating organizational dynamics. There were days, however, when my attempts to build rapport seemed to fall apart. While inevitable, these experiences requires one to develop a thick skin; I learned not to feel personally slighted when doors shut in my face, lunchtime conversations stalled when I walked into the room, or staff stared at me across a meeting room.

Exiting Organizational Research Sites

In all field-based research, there is often no clear way to know when to exit the research site. Researchers frequently make pragmatic decisions based on the resources and time available for the study. My study of local welfare organizations was no different. In my experience, though, there were two distinct types of exit. The first was the period in which I stopped intensive data collection. Because my methodology dictated that I leave open the possibility of additional periods of investigation, however, this exit was tentative. For each site, I did a face-to-face debriefing with the senior manager who had provided initial access to the site, sharing with him or her my initial impressions of key issues. To maintain some connection to the organization, I made periodic phone calls to key informants, to ask clarifying questions and learn about new policy and programmatic developments. When I wanted to reenter the organization for more focused data collection, these key informants were critical in helping me determine appropriate timing and scope. The second type of exit was my decision to leave the site for a final time. At this point, I held more formal debriefing sessions with top management and, in some cases, volunteered to analyze some data concerning pressing organizational problems.

From my experience, each step in the process of accessing human service organizations for field-based research is both rewarding and daunting. It requires a delicate balance of substantive knowledge, interpersonal skill, and research craft. Going through the stages of learning about the organizational field, identifying particular sites, and developing rapport with individuals takes time, emotional energy, and perseverance. However, the lessons that can be learned—for the academic literatures, for your students, for yourself—can be invaluable.

Notes

1. Ann Chih Lin, *Reform in the Making: The Implementation of Social Policy in Prison* (Princeton, N.J.: Princeton University Press, 2000), 177.

2. Fenno, *Homestyle*, 279.

3. Fenno, *Homestyle*, 285.

4. Fenno, *Homestyle*, 283–85.

5. Stalking is illegal in most states.

6. Fenno, *Homestyle*, 285.

7. Lin, *Reform in the Making*.

8. Daniel-Echols, "Mandates, Ideal, and Survival."

9. The publications from this study include the following: Jodi R. Sandfort, "Moving Beyond Discretion and Outcomes: Examining Public Management from the Front-Lines of the Welfare System," *Journal of Public Administration Research and Theory* (October 2000); Jodi R. Sandfort, "The Structural Impediments to Front-Line Human Service Collaboration: Examining Welfare Reform at the Front-Lines," *Social Service Review* 73, no. 3 (September 1999); Jodi R. Sandfort, Ariel Kalil, and Julie Gottschalk, "The Mirror Has Two Faces: Welfare Clients and Front-Line Workers View Policy Reform," *Journal of Poverty* 3, no. 3 (Summer 1999); Jodi R. Sandfort, "Exploring the Structuration of Technology within Human Service Organizations," *Administration & Society* (June 2002); and Jodi R. Sandfort, "Peering into the 'Black Box': A Study of the Front-Line Organizations Implementing Welfare Policy in Michigan," Ph.D. diss., University of Michigan, 1997.

Gaining Access for Extended Observation 9

I N THIS CHAPTER, the researchers in the vignettes featured all gained access for extended observation—at least several weeks—in each of their chosen research sites. What this group of stories has in common is not just a longer period of time spent with their research subjects but also the desire to observe those they were studying in their environments. In addition to conducting interviews, the researchers spent time "hanging around," attended meetings, and were present at informal gatherings. Three of the contributors were even present at social events attended by their research subjects.

To carry out their research designs, researchers often require ingenuity and flexibility. One political scientist conducting an extended observation of elected officials insists that on the campaign trail traditional expectations of how long an interview will take and the conditions in which it will occur no longer govern. "The researcher must go further to accommodate the informant and to get the interview."[1] This is true for those conducting extended observation in any setting where scheduled interviews may have to be postponed when work pressures intervene. In situations like this, researchers are encouraged to be flexible and to take advantage of informants' periods of inactivity.

The researchers whose access stories are described here also asked for permission to observe various actors as they went through their day. It is important to distinguish the process of asking for permission to observe actors from asking for permission to conduct interviews. Accompanying subjects to meetings and other events where the researcher is an outsider frequently involves the informant's explaining the researcher's presence to others unaware of the project, something that one's informants may be hesitant to do. Those who engage in extended observation and want access to a variety of experiences must learn to accept rejection gracefully when a particular experience is closed to them, to remain persistent, and to keep asking to be included.

Extended observation is frequently referred to as "participant observation."[2] What distinguishes this section from the next is that the researchers in this section generally function as "passive" participant observers[3]—their function is mainly to observe rather than to act as a full participant. Despite the fact that all function mainly as passive participant observers, the researchers in this chapter, like those in the previous one, represent a variety of levels of engagement. This can be measured in part by the time spent in the environment and partially through the level of the researcher's interaction with the environment. The experiences of the researcher in the first story, Perlow, who spent seventeen weeks interviewing and observing engineers in China, Hungary, and India, have much in common with stories at the end of the prior chapter. Similarly, another story in this chapter, by Enomoto, describes an entire year conducting fieldwork at school. She did volunteer work in one of the school's offices, and her story has many commonalities with those of the participants whose access stories are described in the next chapter.

Two of the stories in this section, Bell's and Enomoto's, address gaining access to especially challenging bureaucratic public institutions: schools and police stations. Access to specific public institutions with long histories of bureaucracy present some unique challenges not just in obtaining access but also in determining where one is placed within a structure, in utilizing contacts effectively, and in renegotiating access for specific tasks within the institution.

Fading into the Background

One of the goals of those engaged in participant observation is to minimize their presence and thus their effect on the environment. Many researchers aim to blend in with the rest of the environment, to become the proverbial "fly on the wall."[4] We assume that if we disappear as researchers, we have achieved the very height of access, access to information available only to participants. Irrespective of whether this state can actually be achieved, participant observers do their best to assimilate, by dressing like others in the environment, by learning new skills, by remaining silent, and by withholding views they think subjects will find objectionable. Participant observers frequently hide aspects of their identity, their beliefs, sometimes the car that they drive (see Schermer's access story in this chapter), or facts about them that they believe will distance them from those in the site.[5] Sometimes observers fear that access will be taken away if they are too candid about their personal traits. One researcher studying the police hid his liberal ideas: "If . . . I had let my liberal ideas be too well known, or if I'd been openly critical of anything an officer had done, I feared my riding days would be over. To be perfectly frank, I was too anxious to get my Ph.D. to take that risk."[6]

It is unclear whether researchers risk anything at all when they reveal parts of their identities. In her access story, Bell feels that she experienced no change in rapport after a part of her identity that she had tried to keep hidden was accidentally revealed. It may be that some parts of our identity matter more than others. Another police researcher complained bitterly about how being identified as a liberal impeded his access and frequently prevented him from accompanying the detectives outside the office and from viewing events that took place within the office.

> In the author's fieldwork experience, over four and one-half months at one division, he became viewed as a liberal sympathizer with "criminals" among other "underdogs." For example, detectives would often check what they were saying about how suspects were handled, or check racist comments, making reference to the researcher's presence.[7]

For fear of alienating those being studied, shared identity thus becomes an important part of blending in for the participant observer. The more one looks like the rest of the environment, the easier it is to blend in with subjects. "[A]ccess problems are . . . exaggerated when certain of the researcher's ascribed characteristics differ markedly from those of subjects."[8] This was true for one researcher studying adolescent deviants. As an adult (albeit a young one) studying juveniles, the researcher's presence as an outsider was immediately obvious. He deliberately adopted youthful dress—jeans, tennis shoes, old shirts, and sweaters—and was then able to be unobtrusive enough that casual strangers failed to notice him.[9]

Participant observers want to appear as much like their subjects not only because they want the subject to "forget" that they are present and to act normally but also because they believe that similarity between researcher and their informants—even one that is constructed—builds trust. For a participant observer, even a passive one, this means participating in the activities with those one is studying in order to build trust and acceptance. If one is studying the police, that approach may mean carrying a gun when asked to do so,[10] working the car's radio, or keeping the log.[11] The researcher studying deviants whose story was referred to earlier accepted beer offered to him by adolescents and participated in baseball games to fit in and gain the trust of those whom he was studying.

Once trust has been established, those engaged in participant observation must maintain relations and develop rapport. For those engaged in extended observation, rapport becomes "a blend of the external and internal ingredients of day-to-day involvement."[12] Rapport is thus developed over time in the course of interaction, both formal and informal with the informants. The development of rapport may be facilitated when researchers who conduct participant observation try to understand their informants' perspectives by living as they do or otherwise putting themselves in their informants' place. For instance, those engaged in participant observation may try to spend the same amount of time in the office as their informants. In one of the access stories in this chapter, the researcher, Perlow, tried to live like the engineers she was studying, residing in an apartment in their community, shopping in their stores.

When establishing rapport with our subjects, identity matters. As F. C. Mann observed, "[T]he researcher must recognize that . . . his subjects . . . have some bases on which to predict what he will be like and how he will act. These are generally centered around characteristics such as age, sex, race, perceived class, and other factors which have some cue stimulus value."[13] Participant observers, who spend longer periods of time with informants and have more opportunities for interaction than other researchers, sometimes find that "shared identification provides common ground, and therefore, something to talk about during initial encounters."[14] Differences between researcher and informant may increase access as well. One researcher, a midwestern Jewish woman studying seminary students, discovered that her similarities and her differences with others helped secure and maintain a level of interest and built rapport.[15] One contributor in this section, Bell, a black woman, describes being pulled aside by white male officers so she could be told *their* stories.

Researcher or Participant?

The combination of spending long periods of time with subjects and occasionally "helping out" to gain their trust leads to a blurring of the researcher/participant line. The blurring of this line is natural, given the strangeness of the participant-observer role. Participant observers seem to function neither fully as observer—wholly on the sidelines asking questions or otherwise observing—nor as full participants. This sense of role ambiguity may create a sense of unease for participant observers as they attempt to remain detached observers while developing sympathies for and allegiance to the true participants. Fear of losing their objectivity may push observers out the door, where they can safely recover their detachment and reflect on their experiences in the field.

Studying Work Groups in India, China, and Hungary

Leslie A. Perlow

My previous research had focused on time usage among small groups of software engineers working in the United States. I wanted to better understand whether alternative ways of using time exist for people doing the same type of work in different contexts. I therefore decided to study small groups of software engineers working on comparable tasks in different cultures.[16] Ideally, I would have liked one site in Japan and one in Germany: The Japanese have a reputation for working tremendously long hours, and the Germans have a reputation for working relatively short hours. I was eager to explore the work patterns behind these quantifiably different work hours. However, I also knew I might have to be flexible.

Trying to Get Access Abroad

I set out to find both funding and access. I suggested to one colleague that I would study a company with which he was closely connected to the CEO, where they were concerned about cultural differences in their divisions around the world; I suggested studying their operations in several regions. I met with another colleague who suggested India as a possible site. At the same time, I was put in touch with "Research Institute" (a pseudonym), which funds research, but only in transitional economies. Moreover, this organization turned out to be more interested in funding research once one already had access.

Getting Access in India

One afternoon, I told an old adviser about my latest research proposal, expecting endless ideas and advice about what to study and how, but never considering the possibility that this discussion might lead to access. I learned a lesson then about never overlooking anyone who might be able to help. My adviser introduced me to another professor in a very different area (I'll call him Ravi). Ravi was working hard to develop an exchange program and to find scholars who would visit each other's schools. Although my interest was not in finding a foreign school at which to work for several months, I willingly agreed to visit his school in India in exchange for help in gaining access.

When I proposed my research to Ravi, I emphasized how my project might help an Indian company better understand its engineers' usage of time and provide them some comparative data with the United States. After this conversation, I provided Ravi a brief proposal, a one-page synopsis of my previous research, my vita, and a one-page description of what I would need while I was in India in terms of both a research site (my preference was a joint venture with an American-headquartered multinational company) and accommodations (it was important to me to live like the engineers I was studying so I could experience power outages, shopping at the market, commuting to work, etc.).

Finding the right person in the United States to support my research turned out to be key. Decoupling the requests for access and funding also helped. It was much easier to get Ravi's help because I did not need funding from him or anyone in India. At the same time, it was much easier to encourage Research Institute to fund me once I had access.

Pursuing Access at Sites beyond India

Almost immediately after arriving in India, I started thinking about how to gain access to further sites so I could address the research question I had set out to answer. I had intentionally requested to study an Indian company that was part of a joint venture with an American-based multinational. My hope was to spend about two months in India and then move on to joint ventures with the same American company, preferably in Japan and Germany.

While I was in India, I met with the head of software engineering at the company I was studying, and he mentioned that the Japanese subsidiary of the American multinational was currently engaged in a study of how best to work with Indian engineers. I saw this as a potential door into the Japanese subsidiary and asked him about access in Japan, given my new expertise on the workings of Indian software engineers. He agreed to help, but nothing ever came of it.

Also in India, I met with an American of Indian origin who was working on site in India for two years. I hoped that his association with the American headquarters might place him in a position to help me gain access to the Japanese and the German subsidiaries. Unfortunately, it turned out that despite his seniority in India, back in the United States he was too junior a member of the company to have influence in this type of matter. This meeting led only to an invitation to share an evening at his home with his wife and two kids.

The group I was studying was doing work for a German customer. I wondered how I might create a study where the next step would be exploring the work from the customer's side. At least, I thought, that would enable me to continue the research in Germany. However, studying the customer instead of another group of software engineers was less appealing because of the different nature of work itself. I kept this option as a last resort.

While I was in India, a representative from the American headquarters happened to be visiting for two weeks. Unfortunately, at that point I did not find an appropriate time to ask about the possibility of further access. However, several weeks later, after completing my study in India, I had to return to the United States for personal reasons. While there, I called this man and suggested that I might leverage what I had learned in India to explore other regions that were of interest to his division. He invited me to meet with him and his manager in their New York City office. I flew to New York, presented my proposal, and promised them comparative data across India and whatever other sites we chose, if they provided me with access.

After several highs and lows over the course of the next few weeks as the American headquarters attempted to negotiate access, the general manager in

Shenzhen, China, finally agreed to a study. More good news followed. Several days later I got permission to study a group in Hungary.

Developing Rapport

At each of the three sites, I presented my research as an exploration of the ways in which software engineers use their time at work. I provided my contact an overview of my previous research in the United States and shared my curiosity about whether and how the ways of using time in their company would be similar or different. Together (and with the help of the U.S. headquarters) we chose a group for me to study that would be comparable in task assignment, size, and status within the organization to groups I studied at the other sites. In each case, I also requested a small enclosed space near the group selected so I could meet with its members individually, in private, as well as be nearby to observe them collectively at work. I was given in each case either a conference room or a vacant office.

Once the groups were selected, I found in all three cases that the group members welcomed me, willingly shared their work experiences, and accepted my desire to observe them at work. I made it a point to make them feel welcome in my office, to encourage them to tell me when there were meetings and other events that I should attend, and to go to as many lunches and social events as I could. I also encouraged invitations to their homes so I could learn more about their lives outside of work as well. While I was at each site, I tried to work the hours of the engineers I was studying—which turned out to be significantly more at the Indian site than the other two. I also tried to live like the engineers I was studying, living in apartments in their communities, shopping in their stores.

Because of the language barrier in China and Hungary (in India they speak English in the workplace), I would also often ask engineers or managers to come into my office and explain an incident I had observed. In both China and Hungary, about 75 percent of the engineers speak English, and they all seem to understand it. English is the international language of computer programming, which helped minimize communication problems. Still, the biggest issue in China and Hungary was that I could not understand what they were saying when they were communicating as part of the work itself. For that, I had to depend on a translator, whom I had available at all times. Luckily, though, because of my research agenda, my interest was more in *when* they were talking and the general topic than in what exactly they were saying.

In general, I found people more than willing to answer my questions. They were also eager to ask me questions. Their interest came mostly from the fact that I was an American and, better yet, had studied at MIT. The fact that I was a professor at the University of Michigan business school was of little interest. All of the groups I studied were composed of engineers, and to them MIT was a sign I had made it to the top—they did not seem to care that I had studied organizational behavior instead of engineering. They were eager to hear about life in America, particularly at MIT.

Exit

Since I have left, I have tried to stay in touch with the engineers. Before I departed, I exchanged e-mail addresses with all of them. Some of the Indian engineers have come to the United States on work assignments and have called or visited. Several others have remained in e-mail contact. However, beyond these personal communications, I have made no further contact with the companies, other than providing a summary report of my findings.

Reflecting on My Experience

In the course of eight months, I was able to conduct seventeen weeks of field research—eight weeks in India, six weeks in Hungary, and three weeks in China. I spent a large part of that time managing relationships, getting access, and being flexible and willing to go whenever, wherever, and for however long I could be granted access. However, I also managed to collect fascinating data, which has helped me address my research question.

In several ways, getting access outside the United States differed from getting access within the country. First, I was a foreigner, so people I met appeared to be more intrigued in having me visit. Also, in all three cases, I had no direct contact with the organization I was studying when attempting to gain access. For the first part of the research, I found and proposed my project to Ravi; he did the rest. Similarly, negotiating access in China and Hungary, I found and proposed my idea to the U.S. headquarters; staff there did the rest.

My access story is one of luck, persistence, and flexibility. It was great fortune that I met Ravi. He enabled me to get access to the Indian site, which in turn was a powerful lever to get further access. Complemented with my luck was my willingness to keep on trying to get what I wanted—access—but also a willingness to continually redefine exactly where I wanted access.

Accessing Architects in the Auto Industry

Brian Schermer

In searching for a setting to conduct field research on the influence of corporate clients on everyday architectural practice, I looked to the "Big Three" of the U.S.

auto industry: General Motors, Ford, and Chrysler (now DaimlerChrysler). On a practical level, they seemed to be an excellent choice for my study, because their respective corporate headquarters were all within commuting distance from Ann Arbor, where I was living at the time. Also, I could take advantage of numerous connections through the University of Michigan, where I was attending graduate school.

I was hoping to establish sufficient contact with an architectural "community of practice," or group of collaborating professionals, situated within the automobile industry. I wanted to be able to observe their activities and to talk to individual architects about the nature and meaning of their work as it unfolded. I was, however, wary about directly asking for permission for access, because I was afraid of asking for too much too soon. I felt that I first needed to establish good rapport with a member or members of a group. If I could achieve a level of comfort with them and they with me, I thought, I would simply ask for permission to hang around for an unspecified amount of time and blend in until I completed my fieldwork.[17]

Encounters with General Motors

I had been warned that gaining permission to study General Motors could be problematic because of their sensitivity about their operations and proprietary information. I considered my encounter with GM as analogous to seeking an informational interview with a prospective employer. Just to get in the door, I felt that I would need to present myself in such a way that I would be deemed qualified to conduct a study of this type. I touted in my introductory letters both my own work experience as a professional architect and the names of the sources funding my research. In my first letter to the director of facilities engineering at GM (who is a Michigan alumnus), I even tossed in my résumé for good measure. If it was overkill, at least it had the effect of achieving my objective. I got my interview with the director.

I met with the director in his office at GM headquarters. I found him to be a genial man, and he professed an interest in assisting me. He provided a broad overview of the mission of the facilities group, its history, what challenges it faced, and its strategies for overcoming them. He showed me organization charts, which he said I would not be able to keep because of their proprietary nature. At the end of our conversation, I asked for a quick tour around the office. He seemed a bit surprised by this request, as if it were not on our original agenda, but he obliged.

Despite the director's cordiality, at the end of the interview I did not have a good enough sense of the extent of their operations and the boundaries of the community of practice. I suggested to him that it would be worthwhile for me to meet with some of the architectural staff, and he said that it could be arranged.

It took two months to arrange my next meeting with the architectural supervisor (another Michigan alumnus) and then yet another month to meet with two staff architects. When I spoke to these staff architects, I realized that I had hit a dead end in terms of establishing a foothold at GM. The telltale moment was when the staff architects refused to sign a human subjects release form. Here's how I recorded it in my field notes after my interaction with the first architect:

> We began amicably enough, however, when I brought out the draft consent form, the architect clammed up all of a sudden. How did the director and the supervisor respond to this, he wanted to know? Did they sign it? . . . The architect refuses to sign, citing mainly that he does not know what GM legal's policy is toward such things. I explain that it is for his protection, but I suppose that to him it could be used as proof that we actually spoke.

It had taken four months to garner four interviews. I was still struggling to get a handle on the way GM architects think, and I was unsure how to establish a firmer relationship with them. Fortunately, I was simultaneously searching for other architects situated at the other auto companies.

Approaching Ford

I had started more or less at the top management level with GM. At Ford, I worked from the bottom up. An acquaintance of mine hooked me up via e-mail with a young architect (yet another Michigan graduate), who also worked for Ford Land. This architect described his role at Ford and the company's overall building design and construction management approach. He supplied me with a variety of organization charts and other kinds of material (the kinds of documents that GM would not release to me). I also asked for and was given a tour of the workplace. I still needed, however, to talk to someone closer to the top of the organization to provide me with a better overview. I knew of Fred Kozlowski, Ford Land's vice president of facilities, because he had recently received an award from the Michigan chapter of the American Institute of Architects. I chose to introduce myself to Kozlowski by letter. I followed up with a phone call and arranged to meet him for lunch.

We met at Ford Motor Land Services Corporation, and Kozlowski drove me in his company car to a nearby restaurant. While our conversation was amicable and informative, I was at a loss as to what I needed from Kozlowski other than access to his architects. I felt that we had not established sufficient rapport and that such a request was still premature. Then, our lunch ended with something I had been dreading since I began conducting research at the

Big Three. Kozlowski wanted to drive me back to my car, which was parked back at Ford Land. I was driving a Japanese car, and I feared this might be an issue for an American automobile executive. I recorded the event in my field notes:

> I tell him to turn up one of the aisles—then I realize that we have turned up the wrong aisle. I tell him to "stop up there—here is fine." He looks over and sees a blue Saturn with a big maize and blue "M" decal in the window. "Is that your car there with the "M" on it?" "Yeah, well, school spirit and all," I lied. I figured better GM than Toyota.

Accessing Chrysler

My first encounter with Chrysler was much different than what I experienced with GM and Ford. Not only did I find an accessible group of architects, but I also found an unobtrusive parking space for my car.

I had a contact who suggested I speak to Jeff Polachek, who managed the design and construction of a major research facility addition to the Chrysler Technology Center (CTC) in Auburn Hills, Michigan. I contacted Polachek by letter, followed up with a phone call, and set up an appointment. The morning of our meeting, I allotted myself two hours to drive the seventy miles from Ann Arbor to Auburn Hills, but I still arrived forty minutes late. I arrived breathless and apologetic, but the Chrysler people were quite gracious. It turned out that Polachek needed to attend a funeral and that he had arranged for me to meet with Bill Phelan, an in-house architect at Chrysler.

Bill is a cheerful, heavy-set man given to elliptical sentences and the odd malapropism. Nevertheless, he is perceptive, and he was eager to help me understand Chrysler's approach to construction management at the CTC. Bill showed me charts of the various interdisciplinary "field teams" that corresponded to different parts of the construction project. He walked me around the office and showed me where the different team members sat. By virtue of Bill's description and the clarity of the office layout, this practice setting seemed well suited for my study.

My interaction with Bill that morning could not have been more helpful, but Bill was not quite finished with me. He drove me in his pickup truck to the construction site and gave me a tour of the new building and rest of the CTC. I never actually had to ask for permission to come back and observe the Chrysler architects in action. As Bill described the work setting to me, he kept suggesting to me the different types of meetings that I would need to attend, as well as the people with whom I would need to talk. After my cordial but somewhat stilted interactions with architects at Ford and GM, I knew that I had identified an appropriate community of practice.

Over the next months, I attended a variety of meetings at Chrysler, with Bill acting as my personal ambassador and interpreter. He made a point of introducing me to the group at the beginning of meetings and explained what I was doing there. He took it upon himself to point out key players in the meetings. Afterward, he would answer my questions and interpret events for me. He even found a little-used workspace for me to leave my things and write up field notes.

There were some limits to my access. I did not have an ID card, so I always had to sign in with the security guard at the front desk. I also never felt comfortable walking around the construction site without an escort. Once, however, I wanted to attend a ceremony marking the opening of one section of the new building. By the time I got to office, everyone was already at the job site, and I had no one to walk me over. I borrowed a hard hat and just showed up. A few people did a double take, but they took my presence in stride.

Over time, I got to know several of the architects, as well as other people involved with the project. Because Bill had made such a big deal of introducing me, people knew why I was there, and those who were so inclined would stop and chat with me. Others were less approachable. In fact, the construction supervisors were downright gruff. I surmised from their lack of eye contact that they suffered neither fools nor ethnographers gladly. I was satisfied to observe them from a safe distance. After several months, I felt like I was generally accepted, as I had wanted to be.

Leaving the Scene

Eventually, I decided to phase out my fieldwork at Chrysler. The architects I was observing stopped coming to many of the team meetings or at least tended to duck out early. As the Michigan winter weather grew worse, my tolerance for driving the 140-mile round trip to Auburn Hills waned. One morning I awoke to a snowstorm, contemplated the prospect of a long, hazardous commute, and decided that the fieldwork portion of my study was complete.

I feel ashamed about this, but I never went back to Auburn Hills to say thanks in person to the people who helped me. When I was conducting my fieldwork, I would often think about how I wanted to end it. I thought that once I finished my project, I would send Bill Phelan and the rest of them a box of cigars to share. That impulse, however, left me without a plan for staying in touch until I finished my study. Bill had expressed interest in reading my report, but I was reluctant to share it with him or anyone else associated with the study.

I did see Bill Phelan one more time, in the baggage claim area at the Detroit Airport. I was returning from a job interview, and Bill and his wife were coming back from a vacation. He acted very surprised to see me. Then, ever the informant, he told me that one of the Chrysler in-house architects had been taken off the job for poor performance. While Bill was removing his luggage from the carousel, I told his wife that he was a wonderful guy and that he had been incredibly helpful to me. She seemed pleased. I hope she told him I said so.

Access into Rivera:
Entering and Exiting an Urban High School

Ernestine K. Enomoto

Rivera High is a red brick building, a city high school in a low-income, ethnic enclave of a midwestern metropolis. I first entered the building in the spring of 1991 to examine how the school dealt with its high incidence of truancy.[18] Access into the school appeared to be tightly controlled, with guards and a security system. But over time, I came to learn that the guards were not so fearsome, the regulations not strictly enforced, and there was a back door to the parking lot. My access story is about entering Rivera, developing relationships with the people there, and trying to exit gracefully.

Access Carte Blanche
On that first day at the school, I met briefly with the principal, who in turn introduced me to the dean of students, responsible for school attendance. Both administrators welcomed my offer to conduct further research on truancy. I would begin my work the following September and conduct field studies at Rivera throughout the 1991–92 school year. My objective was to define the school's attendance concerns while gathering data to complete a dissertation study on the subject of in-school truancy. Access to the school was relatively easy, a carte blanche.

The ease of access hid several questions and issues that might have been considered prior to commencing a research study. First, was this site the best school to be studying this problem? The school did meet my criteria of interest—namely, it was an inner-city school with an ethnically diverse student population. It was also addressing a school problem with an improvement policy. But was Rivera an exemplary school or otherwise exceptional? How was it unique or similar to other urban high schools? Could I relate my findings to schools facing similar problems? These answers were not clear to me. Given the bureaucracy of the school system, gaining access to any city school would be difficult to obtain. I had had firsthand experience of this in an earlier research study, delayed for several weeks because of failure to gain necessary classroom access. Thus, I decided to proceed with Rivera High, acknowledging its limitations while taking advantage of the access given by the school administration.

A second concern for me was an ethical issue, connecting my ease of access with my university affiliations to an accreditation agency. At the time of my initial visit, Rivera High had recently completed its accreditation process and was awaiting the outcome. While not directly connected with accrediting the school, I was affiliated with the agency in charge of that process. I worked under the accreditation consultant who had expressed concern about attendance problems at Rivera. I wondered whether my easy access was due in part to the school's desire to please that consultant. However, in talking with the principal, I trusted that she had the school's best interests in mind—namely, that my research study might help the school solve its attendance problems. Furthermore, the accreditation visit had been completed, and whatever its outcome, my involvement with the school would have little impact on it. This understanding relieved my own concerns about how easily I had gained access and with whom I was affiliated.

Permission through Paperwork

Another access to the school involved securing the necessary permission to conduct the research. There were two institutions with which to contend: first, the university that authorized my study, and second, the school system. The university required a human subjects approval application, specifying the nature of my study and, more important, that my research would not be harmful to any of the participants. While standard practice, this regulation did require paperwork to be processed in our department, then through the School of Education, and finally at the university level. Various committees at each different level reviewed my study prospectus to grant the necessary permission to proceed, all requiring my time, patience, and persistence.

Negotiating my way through the second institution was even slower. The city school system required that I submit a prospectus as well as agree to submit a final project report. Permission was to be secured first from the school principal and then submitted to the system.

Communication back and forth detailed what was required and by whom. That approval process took nearly a year. Fortunately, I did not hold off my research during this time. Rather, I chose to submit letters while concurrently visiting the school and gathering data. Not until the following spring did I gain official system approval. While it was risky to proceed without written approval, I felt that the principal was the first line of authority for the school system, and, having secured her approval, I would eventually obtain the system authorization if I remained patient yet persistent.

Several professional affiliations and contacts facilitated my gaining access and navigating through the institutional bureaucracies. My initial visit was through my university affiliation with the accreditation agency. The university served to legitimize my presence as a researcher. My working relationship with a former deputy superintendent of the city schools helped me persist and gain the necessary permission from the system. Contacts did help me to access Rivera.

Trust, Rapport, and Relationship

Once inside the doors, an ethnographic researcher begins by developing relationships with the school members. I began by interviewing attendance staff to establish a sense of the operations of that office. There was a formality in my contacts with school personnel. I saw them within their respective roles at school. During the second term, from January to June, I volunteered regularly in the attendance office, doing work similar to that of the parent volunteers who staffed the office. This term-long commitment and regular interaction facilitated the trust building necessary in developing relationships. I was recognized as a member of the attendance office, with work to do and a reason for being there. I was occasionally consulted in attendance matters and, over time, regarded as a colleague and friend.

With my regular presence at school, there were more opportunities to meet people, talk informally, and help out at school. I frequently talked with teachers on hall duty or standing outside their classrooms. During lunch periods, I visited them in teacher lounges or in the lunchroom. Regularly, I went with the school truant officer, a counselor, and some fellows from a nearby high school for lunch at the Polish diner up the street. After school, I chatted with teachers in the tutoring center or outside in the parking lot. In May, when the school sponsored Saturday workshops for students and parents, I voluntarily assisted the staff by helping with registration, directing participants to classrooms, distributing morning snacks, and even making donut runs.

The more I was seen at the school, the more I was able to cultivate relationships with school members. For me, what had begun as a research endeavor did not remain that. I developed relationships with people at school to establish trust and learn more about school concerns, but ultimately it was not strictly for research. I sought to understand the concerns from individual viewpoints—that is, how a single mother dealt with truant youngsters, why older brothers or sisters chose to stay home to help younger siblings, how certain Hispanic teachers assisted nonnative speakers, and so on. During the course of the school year, I developed personal ties with the people there, getting to know them as friends as well as school participants. When the social studies teacher lost his wife to cancer, I offered condolences at the wake. I congratulated the calculus teacher on her summer fellowship. The guidance counselor from our lunch gang announced his retirement, and I joined in celebrating with him at the Polish diner. Sharing the sorrows and celebrating the achievements, I became part of the Rivera school community.

Tamed Subjectivities

Yet another kind of access necessary in conducting qualitative research is access to one's self by identifying and thereby "taming" the numerous subjectivities necessary for a researcher to better understand other people's viewpoints. Taming one's subjectivities was easier to write about than to do. I found that the intersection between others and myself would often blur as I engaged in a social setting with others who were different from yet similar to me. Also, the access to others continued to evolve over time as relationships developed. Two subjectivities that emerged for me in conducting this study related to being an ethnic minority and a former math teacher.

Rivera's student population included 30 percent African American, 30 percent Anglo-American, and 30 percent Hispanic students. As an Asian American, I found myself particularly sensitive to ethnic differences among minorities there. I began by investigating ethnicity as a factor in determining truancy and how the school took action against certain individuals. But this ethnic minority viewpoint tended to overemphasize the activities of those individuals who chose to promote ethnic ties, while it deemphasized those who sought to minimize ethnicity in order to assimilate. Personally, I could relate to some ethnic differences (e.g., acknowledging that Tex-Mex Americans might chose to distinguish themselves from recent immigrants from Central America or the Caribbean). However, I was ignorant of the subtle differences among Hispanic subgroups at the school and the ways that individuals chose to become Americanized.

I held a math teacher's subjectivity, having taught mathematics for two years. My sympathies for this viewpoint were further encouraged as I regularly shared coffee and conversation with the math teachers in their department lounge. I listened to their stories and heard their complaints. The more I visited that group, the more comfortable I felt and the more aligned to their school concerns. I realized that I held a teacher advocacy position when talking with a university colleague. He favored the administrator's position regarding attendance taking, whereas I clearly advocated the teacher's viewpoint. I was less critical of teacher perspectives on student attendance and truancy, and more sympathetic to their needs for fair and consistent treatment of students, than the administrators might have been.

Exiting Gracefully

Eventually the school year came to a close, and I completed my time at Rivera. If access was easy, then so was exiting. But relationships among friends are not so easily closed. I frequently thought about the individuals, worrying about the changes occurring for the staff. Periodically I would call the attendance office or visit for coffee with the math teachers. The ease of access has meant entry into the lives of some wonderful people and a few connections that still remain, even after nearly a decade.

Crossing That Yellow Line:
Obtaining Access to the Police Departments

Jeannine Bell

"Police: Do Not Cross." The familiar yellow and black plastic tape that separates on-lookers from the police at a crime scene serves as an accurate metaphor for researchers who want access to police departments. Though police departments can make it hard for researchers to obtain access, one can get "in," if one is persistent, flexible, and lucky. This account describes how I managed to cut through the yellow tape to study the hate crime unit of a large police department in "Center City."[19]

Getting My Foot in the Door

My research, undertaken as a Ph.D. dissertation, examined how police hate crime units enforce hate crime law. Hate crime units are detective units that investigate racist, antireligious, or antigay and lesbian crimes. My research design required observation of the officers at work, examination of the unit's files, and semistructured interviews with officers and others involved in hate crime law. Though I planned to spend four months in the field, I was granted access initially for only eight weeks. In the end, I spent more than five months in a unit, with an additional two-week trip nine months after my initial visit to clean up the data set.

In my experience, access to police departments is secured from the top—by sending a letter to the chief of police. If the chief's office approves your project, it will send it on to either to the research department or to the unit that is being studied. Experienced police researchers told me that to get access I needed a contact inside the department and a hook. Contacts tell you how to get your research project approved and discuss the likelihood of its approval. If one is lucky, one's contact will inquire about the project as it moves through the approval process.

The hook is simply the reason, from the police department's perspective, that it makes sense to approve your project. A good hook that shows that the department will benefit from letting you in is crucial, as researchers cost the department in man-hours wasted showing researchers around, or watching them.

Even with a hook and a contact, one must be persistent. My first attempt at access ended in failure, even though it was at first approved. After this abortive attempt, I sent my proposal to another department that had shown interest. Though my proposal was well received, I was denied access when the chief to the police abruptly closed the department to all research projects. Having failed at getting in where I had contacts, I happened to see the director of research for the police department of Center City—a city known for its hate crime unit—listed on the program of an academic conference. I approached him after his presentation with my proposal, and he reluctantly agreed to help me write my letter. My letter was sent to the department and forwarded to the head of the unit. After a brief in-person meeting with me a few weeks before the project was scheduled to begin, the unit's supervisor approved the project. I was in.

Negotiating All the Access I Wanted

Though the commander had approved my project, after I arrived I realized there was more to access than just getting in the door. I needed to seek permission for each new type of experience. Even though I was given access to the files, I had to ask each time I wanted to do something new (e.g., make copies of individual files, get copies of documents that were not in the files). In most cases, I had to negotiate access through a sergeant—I'll call her "Nancy"—who was given oversight of my project. For reasons I may never know, Nancy was very supportive of the project, informing me of important activities to see and ensuring my access to nearly every situation I requested. She even helped me get "ride-alongs" in the cars with detectives, something other researchers had suggested might be difficult to obtain.

I also wanted to observe detectives' activities out of the office. The only way I could find out where and when they were going out was to ask them. I had to do this several times a week. This meant I had to get over my fear of being a pest. I learned to ask detectives frequently whether they were going out and whether I could tag along. I was hesitant to do this, because I understood the disincentive in taking me out with them. Some detectives use this time to conduct personal business. Detectives also liked to limit the number of outsiders who might distract the interview subjects. For meetings, unless they took place in the office, I generally waited to be invited. Here, again, Nancy's help was invaluable. She often served as a liaison between the community and the department and took me to many meetings, training sessions, and other events.

My research design also required me to get access to people outside the unit. Making calls from the unit boosted my credibility with outsiders. I met many of the lawyers and victim advocates I interviewed either through a police department contact—Nancy introduced me to several at a conference—or through the snowball method. At the end of the interview I asked respondents to give names of others they felt would be helpful. This allowed me to generate names and also to have the name of someone who could "vouch" for my credibility.

Rapport and Identity

Most of the detectives in the unit seemed comfortable with my presence, perhaps because I spent so much time in the office. To observe detectives on both the day and the night shifts, most days I came to the office in the late morning and stayed until the late evening. The willingness to put long hours in the office and accompany officers when nothing exciting was happening often surprised and sometimes impressed officers. They noticed my commitment to learning about their world. Just two weeks into the fieldwork, for instance, there was a retirement party for the person who'd been head of the unit for a number of years. The ticket for the event was expensive. The veteran officer who sold me the ticket could not believe I would "pay so much to go to the retirement dinner of someone I'd never met."

When detectives saw me taking an interest in what they were doing, they stopped treating me like a guest and slowly began to ask what I thought about events. After about a month in the unit, detectives began to ask me whether I wanted to accompany them on investigations or to events. Some officers showed how comfortable they were with my presence by confiding their frustrations about others in the unit, or those outside, to me. Others talked to me about their families or other issues unrelated to work.

Part of building rapport with the detectives meant that I had to swallow my pride and allow them to see me in a way that was comfortable and made sense to them—someone who was young, inexperienced, and naïve, a student. Outside the office, the detectives called me an "intern," a term they adopted to explain my presence to others in a way that did not invite questions or complaints from outsiders. This image conflicted with the skilled professional visage I was used to as a researcher, legal consultant, and teacher of undergraduates. I had to resist my natural urge to fight their characterization and prove that I was competent. Not being considered a *serious* researcher meant that members of the unit often volunteered explanations for the curious or confusing and took pains to take me places to expose me to parts of the job they considered significant. While my ego may have suffered a bit in the beginning, what I gained as a result of their explanations more than made up for it.

My two most open informants were a black woman and a white man. I think I developed rapport with black and white, male and female detectives for different reasons. My race and gender—I'm an African American woman—may have suggested to the black and female detectives (who were quicker to volunteer stories about their work and lives) that I might better appreciate their perspective. Though I behaved the same toward detectives of both races, white detectives may have inferred that I was open to them because I listened to their stories without judgment. Still other detectives noticed my being taken aside and worried that their views would not be represented in the study, so they made sure they talked to me.

While useful at building rapport, the combination of my gender and age may have limited my access to some situations. Male police researchers tell stories about holding a gun or other exposure to dangerous situations. Perhaps because of my age and gender, detectives excluded me from any situation in which they thought they might face danger. Because I was studying detectives who rarely encountered dangerous situations, my access to situations I felt I needed to observe was not impeded.

At the same time I was trying to get detectives to open up in order to learn how they viewed their work, I endeavored to hide my background and views. As is standard in my profession, I did my best to keep every aspect of my identity hidden—especially those I felt would distance me from these largely working-class cops. I was most guarded about my liberal political beliefs, my upper-middle-class background, and my Ivy League education, for I believed that my subjects would be more honest if they assumed they were talking to a blank slate.

Concealing that much of myself was very hard to do for long. By mistake, three or four months into my research I wore my college signet ring to the unit. Within five minutes of my arrival that day from four feet away, a detective spotted my ring. He bellowed, "Is that a Harvard ring? Is that *your* ring?" I blushed, did not say a word, and was subject to immediate teasing. Though later the detective threatened to reveal to the entire unit "where I really came from," as he called it, another detective who had already learned where I went to college prevented him from "blowing my cover."

In retrospect, I am skeptical about whether hiding aspects of one's identity is required to obtain the information that one desires, and about whether it is even possible. My dress (professional, like the detectives), my pursuit of advanced degrees, my ability to spend several months studying the unit while not working at all marked me as upper middle class. I learned later that some of the detectives assumed (erroneously) that my father was a judge. Since my efforts to conceal my class background totally were unsuccessful, perhaps they were unnecessary. While the ring incident was embarrassing, my respondents acted no differently toward me after it.

Exit

Deciding to leave was complicated for me because I had had such difficulty getting in. In the end, the worry that I might go "native," as well as logistical issues, pushed me out. When I left, I told Nancy that I would like to return in a few months to clean up the data set. I maintained contact over the intervening months with Nancy. Even though I had prepared, reentry was not a given. The commander who had initially approved the project was promoted, and my reentry had to be approved by the new commander. Luckily, I was allowed to return.

Doing this research allow me to cross the yellow tape and placed me with the detectives, on the other side of the tape from civilian onlookers. I even had an identification badge that granted me physical access to offices and distinguished me from the civilians who visited police headquarters. Having completed the project, I am firmly in the civilian world and no longer straddling that yellow tape.

Notes

1. See James M. Glaser, "The Challenge of Campaign Watching: Seven Lessons of Participant Observation Research," *PS, Political Science & Politics* 29 (September 1996): 534.

2. R. F. Ellen, "Producing Data," in *Ethnographic Research: A Guide to General Conduct* (London: Academic Press, 1984), 217. For examples of use of the term to refer to a variety of different level of involvement in the informants' lives, see, generally, George McCall and J. L. Simmons, *Issues in Participant Observation* (London: Addison-Wesley, 1969); William Shaffier, Robert A. Stebbins, and Allan Turowetz, *Fieldwork Experience: Qualitative Approaches to Social Research* (New York: St. Martin's, 1980); Glaser, "The Challenge of Campaign Watching."

3. See McCall, *Issues in Participant Observation*, 96.

4. See Ellen, "Producing Data."

5. See Glaser, "The Challenge of Campaign Watching," 536. He advises, "Reveal your purpose, suppress your opinions."

6. Howard Pepinsky, "A Sociologist on Police Patrol," in *Fieldwork Experience: Qualitative Approaches to Social Research*, ed. William Shaffier, Robert A. Stebbins, and Allan Turowetz (New York: St. Martin's, 1980), 228.

7. Richard V. Ericson, *Making Crime: A Study of Detective Work* (Toronto: Butterworths, 1981), 32.

8. W. Gordon West, "Access to Adolescent Deviants," in *Fieldwork Experience: Qualitative Approaches to Social Research*, ed. William Shaffier, Robert A. Stebbins, and Allan Turowetz (New York: St. Martin's, 1980), 31.

9. West, "Access to Adolescent Deviants," 38.

10. See Jerome Skolnick, *Justice without Trial* (New York: Wiley, 1962).

11. Pepinsky, "A Sociologist on Police Patrol," 229.

12. Shaffier et al., eds., *Fieldwork Experience*, 185.

13. Sherryl Kleinman, "Learning the Ropes as Fieldwork Analysis," in *Fieldwork Experience: Qualitative Approaches to Social Research*, ed. William Shaffier, Robert A. Stebbins, and Allan Turowetz (New York: St. Martin's, 1980), 179.

14. Kleinman, "Learning the Ropes," 180.

15. Kleinman, "Learning the Ropes."

16. Leslie Perlow and John Weeks, "Who's Helping Whom: Layers of Culture and Workplace Behavior," *Journal of Organizational Behavior* 23 (2002): 345–61; Leslie Perlow, "Time to Coordinate: Towards an Understanding of Work Time Standards and Norms in a Multi-Country Study of Software Engineers," *Work and Occupations* 28 (February 2001): 91–113; Leslie Perlow and Jody Hoffer-Gittell, "Dynamic Alignment: The Relationship between Structures and Emergent Networks," unpublished manuscript.

17. This research was undertaken as part of the author's dissertation (currently in progress): "Client-Situated Architectural Practice: Designing and Building the Chrysler Technology Center." Preliminary findings are published in Schermer, "Architectural Communities of Practice: A Preliminary Investigation of a Source of Professional Identity," *Constructing Identity: Proceedings of the 86th ACSA Annual Meeting & Technology Conference, Association of Collegiate Schools of Architecture* (1998): 684–89.

18. Ernestine Enomoto, "In-School Truancy Truancy in a Multiethnic Urban High School Examined through Organizational Lenses," Ph.D. diss., University of Michigan, 1993; Ernestine Enomoto, "Negotiating the Ethics of Care and Justice," *Educational Administration Quarterly* 33, no. 3 (August 1997): 351–70; Ernestine Enomoto, "Schools as Nested Communities: Sergiovanni's Metaphor Extended," *Urban Education* 32, no. 4 (November 1997): 512–31.

19. Jeannine Bell, *Policing Hatred: Law Enforcement, Civil Rights, and Hate Crime* (New York: New York University Press, 2002).

Gaining Access for Participation

10

THIS CHAPTER deals with researchers who become members of the organization they are studying. This is what Adler and Adler call the *complete-member-researcher*.[1] Their description is appropriate:

> Rather than experiencing mere participatory involvement, complete-member-researchers (CMRs) immerse themselves fully in the group as "natives." They and their subjects relate to each other as status equals, dedicated to sharing in a common set of experiences, feelings, and goals. As a result, CMRs come closest of all researchers to approximating the emotional stance of the people they study. CMRs' genuine commitment to the group, and the members' awareness of this, diminishes the need for role pretense. In conducting their research, the, CMRs often adopt the overt role.

The challenges confronted by researchers in the previous chapters are often present in this research. Researchers must often find and develop trusted informants, understand the organizational context, and present themselves as serious researchers and deal with ambiguous boundaries. But this form of research also confronts the researcher with new challenges. These researchers dramatically alter their day-to-day life often for considerable periods of time. They truly adopt a new identity, sometimes, as discussed later in this chapter introduction, to the extent of permanently leaving the old one.

There are many ways to become a member-researcher. Sometimes people study an organization or group to which they already belong.[2] Adler and Adler refer to these people as *opportunistic researchers*.[3] Other times people become members as they study a setting.[4] Adler and Adler refer to these as *converts*.[5] Other researchers actively become members to study the organization or group.[6] At times it is not so clear whether membership or study is primary.[7]

Advantages and Disadvantages of Membership for Access

Regardless of the reason for being a member, membership has advantages and disadvantages for research. Coy describes these aptly: "Occupancy of this role limits what the anthropologist may do, but at the same time the role opens to investigation a wide range of feelings and sentiments that are not accessible to outsiders."[8] The member-researcher comes to understand what motivates people and what constrains their actions because those motivations and constraints either are or become taken for granted by the researcher. What is or becomes taken for granted can be difficult to study. Being so close to the phenomenon that it is hard to see is often, however, better than being so far away that the phenomenon is imperceptible.

One of our contributors, Michael Pratt, has developed a way of thinking about access that helps to understand the advantages provided by membership. He analyzes access along two dimensions: *distant-close* and *surface-deep*.

> The first dimension is more physical, and involves whether access is primarily observational (seeing/distant) or action-oriented (doing/close). The second dimension is more cognitive-emotional. It deals with how much of one's self or how many of one's roles are involved in access. When one's access involves few roles that rarely blend together, I refer to that as surface access. Deep access involves drawing upon "more" of one's self—it demands engaging multiple and "blurring" roles. Becoming a participant helped achieve two "close" forms of access: *close and deep* and *close and surface*. The former is akin to "going native" and involves actually becoming a full participant—emotionally, cognitively, and behaviorally— in the community. The latter involves taking the role of an organizational member, but does not involve full cognitive or emotional participation. In this type of access, you are neither truly an "insider" nor an "outsider." In addition, I gained two types of distant access (1) *distant and surface* access to the organization via news reports, company documents, and other forms of archival data; and (2) *distant and deep* access primarily via interviewing. Distant forms of access allowed me to get the "big pictures" and "rough sketches" of the community I studied, and allowed me to get a type of understanding that comes with *seeing*. The closer forms of access provided me with the "fine grained details" about and the "rich portraits" of participants. They allowed me understanding through *doing*.[9]

The movement from surface to deep in this form of research is often related to time. Over time, people become more involved in the membership role and are able to see different things. This is similar to any apprenticeship.[10] As described by Lave and Wenger in their discussion of legitimate peripheral participation, "learning as increasing participation in communities of practice concerns the whole person acting in the world."[11] As researchers engage with the community of practice, their ability to remain peripheral or superficial decreases. This shift alters what they do, and changing what they do alters what they know. Member-researchers often deal with this by keeping careful notes at the beginning of their fieldwork so that they can return to these and remember what it was like to see things from an outsider's perspective.

Insider and Outsider?

The tension between insider and outsider roles is one striking aspect of this form of research. Member-researchers often feel it is difficult to stay "neutral" within the confines of the participatory role and that their own sense of being researchers was often challenged. The researchers whose access stories are presented in this section all found themselves participating in ways that were clearly inconsistent with a "neutral and objective" researcher stance. They ran meetings, they participated in office politics, they created projects, and they *cared* about what they were doing.

The role of organizations in this research is important in the four selections presented in this chapter. An acceptance of the shifting nature of organizational membership can make it easier to become a member of an organization than it would be to become a member of a community or an individual with a particular cultural orientation. Three of the authors in this chapter used professional expertise they had developed in other contexts in the organization in which they studied and participated. There were a variety of different organizations they each could have joined, and in each of these settings, people routinely moved in and out of organizations. Movement in and out of the fourth setting, Amway, was also common, though current members saw it as deviant.

The ability to move in and out of the setting may raise questions about researcher-membership. Are you really a member if you have become a member to study the organization and plan to leave after a period of time? These questions are reasonable. Even in studies, such as Ehrenreich's *Nickel and Dimed* or Rose's *Black American Street Life: South Philadelphia 1969–1971*, in which the authors took on identities for defined periods of time, what we learn from these studies may omit some important aspects of the experience, but they tell us far more than we could learn otherwise. Yet, clearly, there must be differences between the feelings of people who have no option to leave and those who can leave. The ability to leave, however, does not always mean that one *will* leave. Michael Rosen, a sociologist who wrote several ethnographic articles, after a stint studying Wall Street decided that Wall Street provided a more attractive career opportunity and left to pursue a career as a broker.[12]

Thus, the role ambiguity discussed in the previous chapter becomes acute in this form of research. Though researchers may start the research with clear senses of themselves as researchers, the identities often shift during the course of the fieldwork. The people who wrote these access stories truly belonged to two worlds, and, at times, it was not at all clear which identity was dominant. Certainly on a day-to-day basis, the organizational member identity is often dominant. All of the researchers whose stories are included in this chapter seriously entertained from time to time during their fieldwork the possibility of a permanent shift in identity. For the time being, all of the people who wrote these access stories are more involved in their academic identities than in the alternatives that were generated from their membership in the organizations they studied. This is not necessarily the final outcome for these researchers. In some cases, the ambiguity continues.

Perseverance Furthers

JoAnn M. Brooks

My interest in research on organizational memory grew out of my experience as a software developer. So, too, did my interest in ethnography, a research method commonly used in studies of computer-supported cooperative work. And I had heard that the key to getting ethnographic access in an organization was having insider contacts that knew and *trusted* me. Since I had worked in the software industry and knew many of its people, that seemed the natural place to look for a site. My intent was to find a position as a participant-observer so I could collect data over an extended period of time while also supporting myself with a salary. Actually getting this to happen took several different approaches, more than a few false starts, some luck, and a deep willingness to persevere.

Different Approaches, False Starts

I drove back home from school with my belongings in a seventeen-foot U-Haul truck with car in tow. Upon arriving, I put my things into storage and moved into a friend's guest room—just for a month or so, we thought. I drafted a résumé and started scanning the help-wanted ads to get a sense of what options might exist. What I found was that my skill set and research goals did not match any of the advertised positions. While I had been away at school for five years, the local information technology (IT) industry had gone through its own set of transformations: *Internet* had become a household word, dot-com startups were proliferating, and knowledge management had emerged as a new trend.

To get back in the swim of things, I took advantage of every available opportunity to meet with friends and associates: over lunch and coffee, at professional society meetings, academic seminars, and conferences. Though none of these friends and associates was hiring, they provided many leads toward projects and managers that might be.

My major challenge then was how to prioritize and pursue the available leads. In essence, this problem was a marketing one. Market research (i.e., lots of trial and error) was required before I could figure out how to package my identity, skills, and research agenda into something that would both appeal to hiring managers and permit me reasonable observational access. My former identity as a software developer, back again in the context of a "Silicon Alley" culture, led many people (often including myself) to assume that my research was oriented toward the design of new technologies. While such assumptions facilitated entry into conversations concerning jobs and access, the drawbacks of this approach gradually became apparent. I slowly discovered not only that my interests had shifted from software design to social theory but that a tension between these research goals was not easily resolved in the business context. This tension appeared as a cumulative sense of disappointment at being unable to continue conversations past enthusiastic beginnings.

As my early efforts to construct a marketable package were not very successful, I spent a lot of time rewriting my dissertation proposal, trying to smooth over this tension and sell my research on organizational memory more directly to the business audience (e.g., inserting terms such as *effectiveness*). But the link between my research interests and business value-added remained more remote than the next quarter's earnings, and I was having difficulty justifying my research agenda against the fast-paced IT industry's sensitivity to bottom-line returns. And when I did speak directly with hiring managers, we ended up at cross-purposes, because my admitted interest in research access was perceived by them as opposed to their need for someone who would assume their business goals with total commitment. What was even worse, in trying to compromise this tension I sometimes found myself at risk of promising more than I could deliver, thus placing in jeopardy the reputations of those who had facilitated my initial contacts. Suddenly, maintaining the trust of my friends and associates appeared infinitely more important than building rapport with little-known hiring managers. I retreated into caution and conservatism.

My prospects were looking bleak. I had been in back in town for over two months and still hadn't set foot inside an organization for more than a few hours. Meanwhile, financial worries were growing. I soon started temping as a secretary at a large professional services firm; this job enabled me to pay some bills and got me inside a large organization. Yet I did not believe that I could legitimately use any of these observations without first obtaining the firm's consent. Later I found out that any observations gained in the course of doing my job would be considered ethically obtained, but I did not know this at the time. So after a month of unofficial observation with a few field notes and believing I had established some trust, I asked managers there whether it was permissible for me to collect data. They responded that company policy prohibited disclosing any information about their business practices, and to underscore the point, they recommended that I consider that my last day at the firm! I was crushed.

Fortunately, some good things happened soon after. One associate advised me to write a *short* (five pages maximum) statement of my research topic and design, oriented toward people with interest but not familiarity in my research area of organizational memory. Although this did not open any doors immediately, it renewed my hope and came in useful later on. Miraculously, an unexpected chunk of financial support came through. And one of my dissertation advisers advised me to quit the job search altogether and begin interview-based research instead. I put together an interview protocol, secured IRB approval for it, and soon was interviewing friends, associates, and contacts of contacts. I had given up trying to find a participant observation opportunity altogether, and my morale improved considerably.

Changing Luck

These interviews were going reasonably well and brought me back into contact with several associates who had provided leads earlier. Much to my surprise, one of them, Raul,[13] set up a job interview for me at the research and development (R&D) division of the systems integration organization where he worked, which I call "Megatech." After all my previous failures, I was skeptical but still wanted to give it a try. This job interview process turned out to be quite demanding: In addition to preparing and delivering a job talk on previous research, I had individual meetings with twenty people at the organization. Fortunately, Raul had advised me on how to present myself, what to say to whom, and other tips. In keeping with his advice, I described myself as a researcher with a strong background in human-computer interaction (HCI). In fact, I was beginning to recognize my HCI experience as a key feature of my marketing package; also fortunately in this context, the term *researcher* was broad enough to encompass both my dissertation goals and many of Megatech's R&D concerns. Furthermore, because Megatech is an R&D environment, people there saw no problem with my request for research access (!).

Things were looking good. My job interviews had gone well, and my three-page description of research agenda was well received. Perhaps most important, Raul had been cultivating support for me inside the organization. Within a couple of days, they were prepared to make me an offer.

Less than a week later however, their department was put through a "reorg," and the person who would have been my reporting manager was transferred out of the division. Six weeks later, in spite of continuing assurances, no offer was yet in sight. Meanwhile, my efforts toward this job opportunity had derailed my focus on collecting data through interviews. I was now in genuine crisis. The generosity of friends, family, and credit cards had supported me for almost nine months, and all were now strained to the limit. Changing tack once again, I negotiated for a teaching assistantship back at school for the upcoming term. Once this was in place, I made a last-ditch call to the organization asking for a definite response. This time a real offer came through. My job there started more than two months after the initial interview with them and more than nine months after I'd initiated my search.

On the Inside

Once inside Megatech, things were considerably different. As sometimes occurs in R&D environments, my job was pieced together with bits and pieces from various projects across a range of departments. Raul notified me of research or work opportunities he thought I might find interesting; other managers also suggested potential work assignments. Once I learned my way around, I found it relatively easy to meet people and inquire about what they were working on. If initial discussions revealed complementary interests and capabilities, the conversation sometimes naturally turned to how I could become involved in their project. Megatech's organizational culture generally encourages people to seek out projects that interest them; this tendency, combined with my motivation to observe and participate in many different parts of the company, led to a profusion of research-worthy opportunities.

In all, I managed to develop working relationships with nine different groups of people distributed across several divisions and locations of the company, and I worked on fourteen different projects with very diverse responsibilities.[14] Partially because of my industriousness in this regard, my position also was a high-stress one. After twelve months of working the job and writing field notes on a daily basis, I was too exhausted to continue. Coinciding with a cyclic downturn in the company's business, I scaled back my hours and took a month's rest before slowly beginning to focus on data analysis and writing. As of this writing, I'm now focused full-time on finishing my dissertation,[15] though I'm also still on Megatech's books as a part-time consultant. I hope to return briefly to collect more data through formal interviews.

Megatech has expressed interest in my returning after I complete my degree, and my current plans are to do just that. The challenges of gaining initial access, collecting data, writing a dissertation, and supporting myself all the while have accumulated to more than enough stress for the time being without adding another job search. Of course, at some point in the future I may decide to leave the organization for a position elsewhere, possibly even in academe. Our current arrangement leaves time to prepare for such a possibility, and if/when I do leave, my departure will be as a valued employee as well as a principled researcher.

In the meantime, I keep my academic research separate from any research I do as part of my job description. This approach was recommended by our division director, and it works quite well. I am able to study different topics for each venue, adhere to appropriate standards of quality for each, and stay free of conflicts over time, data, and ownership of ideas.

Looking Back

In retrospect, the key things that enabled me to find participant observation access include maintaining trust of friends and associates who could be helpful; gaining clarity about intersections of observational requirements, skills, and the job market; a *brief* research description oriented toward the anticipated audience; and going ahead with data collection through interviews (good for morale and credibility in addition to data). And, of course, lots of luck and perseverance.

Inside the Department of Energy

Martha S. Feldman

In 1979, I started work on my dissertation research on the process of information production and its relation to decision making.[16] I was interested in garbage-can theories of decision making and whether they were as helpful in explaining decision making in organizations that deal with science and engineering as they had been in organizations that dealt with "soft technologies," such as education, where there were no "right" answers. I decided that the U.S. Department of Energy (DOE) in Washington, D.C., would be a good place to do my study.

Getting In

I moved to Washington, D.C., in the late summer of 1979 to begin my quest. I knew that I wanted to watch the day-to-day activities of people working in the department, but I had no idea how I would gain this kind of access. Eventually, I started interviewing. Gaining access for interviews was not difficult. I found that civil servants believe that part of their job was to talk to people from the public about what they were doing. They were busy, but they often made time to talk with people whom they deemed serious.

Presenting oneself as a serious researcher is important to gaining interview access. Aspects of identity are important. I had a fellowship at the Brookings Institution, which as a liberal think tank was highly regarded by people in the Carter administration. When I called from the Brookings Institution to make appointments, my calls were returned quickly, and I easily set up interviews. When I arrived at the interview, I explained that I was a student from Stanford University working on my dissertation. This pointed to another affiliation with a respected institution and engagement in an understandable and respectable activity.

I also explained my research interests in a way that people could relate to. I did not discuss garbage-can theories or use scholarly jargon. I told them that I was interested in how information is used for decision making. I expressed interest in such questions as how information influences what people think about an issue; whether it matters if the information is solicited or unsolicited; why some information is incorporated into reports and other information is left out. People were not interested in a detailed research design; they wanted to know that I was interested in questions that they thought were important.

As I interviewed, I kept my eyes open for ways that I could spend more time hanging around. At the time I would have accepted anything—stuffing envelopes or photocopying—that would have allowed me to be there every day. In fact, I was beginning to lose hope of being able to do the research in the DOE. I started looking for positions in other organizations when my DOE break came in April 1980. I was in the subway in downtown Washington when I ran into one of the people I had interviewed. He was an assistant director in the Office of Policy Planning and Analysis—we'll call him Mr. Smith. He was in charge of the area that analyzed fossil fuels, oil, gas and coal. He was in a rush, as he always was, and had also just found out that one of his policy analysts was quitting. The policy analyst had held a Brookings fellowship when he had been hired at the DOE. Mr. Smith, remembering that I also had a Brookings fellowship, decided on the spot (in the subway) that I would be a good policy analyst to take his place. I did not point out to him that the other analyst was an economist and that I was a political scientist. I think I stuttered something like, "Are you sure?" and "I'd love to." We agreed to talk about it early the following week.

By early the next week, I had realized that I did not want to go in under false pretenses and that I did not necessarily want all of the constraints of a full-time job, though working as a policy analyst would clearly provide me with incredible access to information and would give a perspective that I could not obtain otherwise. I talked with Mr. Smith and made clear to him what my background was and also that my primary interest was in gathering data for my dissertation. I explained that I would need some time away from the office to be able to write up my notes and to make sense of what I was observing. Mr. Smith assured me that this would be no problem, that I would be able to do the work and still have time for my own work.

Having come to this agreement, I was hired. I was the new policy analyst for coal transportation policy—a job I had never done before and a topic I knew nothing about. I was told to report to the personnel office and start work the next week. The following Monday, I spent the better part of a day filling out forms and being fingerprinted. I still did not totally believe that I had really been hired. It seemed both too good and too bizarre to be true. But I went upstairs to my new office. The previous policy analyst was still there, waiting for me. He had created a stack of reports about two feet high that I should read to familiarize myself with the issues of coal transportation. He showed me the stack and left.

Staying In

My identity quickly changed from graduate student to policy analyst. Several factors influenced this change. One was that a couple of months after I was hired, Mr. Smith left for a job in the oil industry. He was replaced by a senior analyst in our department who had only a vague knowledge of the understanding I had worked out with Mr. Smith. A few months later, Ronald Reagan was elected president. After Reagan's inauguration, new people were placed in managerial positions even down to the level of my boss. My new boss had no understanding of the arrangement that had been made. Even though I made no attempt to hide my status as graduate student, and I explained to him several times the arrangement that Mr. Smith and I had made, he never did understand. Indeed, for the next year, he puzzled over why I was not interested in upward mobility.

Contacts with my peers also influenced my identity. I was almost immediately involved in writing a reported mandated by Congress that had to be signed by the secretaries of energy and transportation. The analysis had been going on for years, and the two departments were at loggerheads in their perspectives on several key issues. But the deadline was approaching, and a report had to be produced. Despite my novice status, I was *the* representative from the policy office, an important component of the DOE team. The position was compelling. As people turned to me to make sure that the policy office would sign off on particular aspects of the report, I found myself becoming the policy analyst they thought they were dealing with.

I did not conceal my reasons for being at the DOE. In fact, from time to time when something particularly funny or egregious would happen, someone would hit their fist on the table and proclaim, "This is one for your book, Martha!" Although they knew that I was working on my dissertation, they saw me fully as a peer and a policy analyst. One indication of this was that they recommended me for other positions as they came open in other parts of DOE, other government departments, and private industry. These opportunities caused some of the most difficult personal moments during the research. I found my dual status very confusing and often wanted to respond as a policy analyst rather than a researcher.

Being an insider had many advantages. I did not have to chase around making sure that I knew of and could attend relevant events; rather, I was a key participant in them. While my perspective was limited (perhaps even more than it always is), I saw whatever *could* be seen from this perspective. There are, however, drawbacks to the insider status. People talked to me, but they talked to me in my role as policy analyst. The processes were quite political, involving the brokering of different interests in relation to the topic at hand. I came to learn the positions of other people, but not as an impartial (or disinterested) observer. My role was necessarily as politically charged as anyone else's.

Even when I talked with and later interviewed people who were "on the same side" of the issues as I was, there were still drawbacks to the insider role. One of the main drawbacks was that I lost some of my right to ignorance. When I interviewed people, I frequently heard the phrase "Oh, Martha, you know how it is." I did have some success with responses such as "Well, can you tell me how it is for you?" but the interviews were very different from those I have conducted with people who know that I am truly unfamiliar with the work that they do. In that sense, I had less access to some information that I would have as an outsider.

The High Cost of Being an Insider

On the whole, insider status was a definite plus in terms of providing access to information. It was, however, a high-cost approach to data gathering. One of the costs was time. Despite my agreement with Mr. Smith, I spent the majority of my time every day and week working as a policy analyst. I regularly woke up at 5 A.M. to do field notes for two hours before getting ready to go to work. By the time I returned in the evening, I seldom had the energy to work on my dissertation. Taking the job seriously, it turned out, was what provided access for me—access to interesting situations but also access to the policy analyst that I had become.

The insider access was also costly in terms of total time that I engaged in data gathering. I held my position as a policy analyst in the DOE for one year and nine months. While I have used information from all of the period of time, I might have been able to leave the organization earlier with sufficient data if I had not also been involved as an insider.

Exit

Leaving was difficult. The work was very engaging. I had also developed relationships with people whom I enjoyed and cared about. Both the work and the relationships were not easy to leave. Leaving was made possible by the fact that my university was across the country and both I and the people I worked with understood that I needed to return there to finish. I promised that I would send copies of my dissertation. I did, in the end, send a copy to the DOE library, and I sent letters to the people I had worked with and interviewed to let them know it was there.

Though leaving was difficult, working with the data within the first six months of leaving was even harder. Every time I started to work with my field notes after leaving, it was as if the entire setting reconstituted itself. I missed the friends and work I had left. Moreover, the depth of my knowledge of the research setting made it difficult to summarize what might be useful to theorists interested in particular aspects of the experience. A quick glance at the field notes could wash away any themes I had begun to develop in a flash flood of memories and feelings.

When I look back on my experience of gaining access, I have to attribute the extraordinary level of access primarily to persistence, serendipity, and availability. For approximately eight months I made myself known to people in the setting and sought positions that would allow me to observe work on a day-to-day basis. At this point, luck plays a major role both in the policy analyst deciding to leave his position and in my running into his boss in the subway station. Once offered the position, I was able to take it and to stay in it long enough to gain a deep understanding of the role of information production in decision making.

Access as Relating: On the Relationship Aspects of Different Types of Access

Michael G. Pratt

As I can best reconstruct, my initial interest in studying Amway distributors came during a trip to my family home several years ago. Amway is a network marketing organization where independent contractors (i.e., distributors) sell products and services outside a central business location.[17] My sister had recently become a distributor, and she was uncharacteristically positive about an Amway-related seminar she had recently attended. As we talked about the seminar and her experiences as a distributor more generally, it became clear that my serious, critically thinking, and extremely independent sister was now a highly excited, "sold out to the system" distributor whose main function was to support her husband in distributing soap, "dreams," and other products and services. She had clearly changed to fit how married couples work together in Amway. Married men are the ones who "show the plan" and recruit others. Married women, by contrast, often engage in support tasks such as bookkeeping, answering the phone, and providing emotional support for their husbands.

She had changed in other ways as well. Although many of the changes were positive, they were nonetheless dramatic and therefore unnerving. I became curious about the organization on multiple levels. On a personal level, I was interested in and concerned about an organization that caused such a personality change in my sister. Professionally, the organization appeared to fit very well with my research interests—which centered on organizations that have powerful ideologies and create strong member attachments. At the time, I was also looking for a research site for my dissertation. Thus, it seemed like wonderful and fortunate coincidence that my personal and research interests would come together so nicely.

Becoming a Member

My curiosity piqued, I began to read more and more about Amway. Thereafter, I attended an Amway-sponsored seminar and soon began to talk with people both inside and outside Amway. Early in this process, it became clear that surveys, unobtrusive observations, and even interviews would not provide the answers to the questions I was asking. This was clearly an identity-transforming organization, and I wanted to know—as a "social scientist," as a doctoral student, and as a concerned family member—*how* it changed people. I therefore decided to become a distributor myself.

Actually joining—buying the starter kit and signing the proper papers—allowed me full access to Amway seminars, rallies, and other events. It also gave me some legitimacy; I was not just a researcher, I was "one of them." But even joining did not give me the access that I really needed to understand fully the hearts and minds of distributors. Gaining the understanding I desired only came through more intensive "doing"—through actually distributing (not just being a distributor). Distributing involved taking on a new role—as someone who sells products, recruits new members, and otherwise participates in the life of distributors. It also involved making new linkages between this role and several other roles.

Making these linkages was challenging but often yielded new insights. For example, as a distributor I was asked to suspend disbelief and to "sell out to the system"—to follow uncritically the advice of those who had sponsored me. As a researcher, by contrast, I was asked to examine, dissect, and otherwise think critically about my experience. The strain of going back and forth between these two roles was great at times, and I spent many a night chronicling these tensions in my research journal. Because of this tension, I greatly limited contact with my academic colleagues during the final months of my study. I later used this experience of needing to separate my "Amway life" from my non-Amway one to help me understand better "closet distributors"—individuals in Amway who had not told friends, family, or coworkers about their involvement. One of these aforementioned distributors was a friend of mine who, upon hearing that I was a distributor, would admit to me his own involvement in Amway only when we were alone (and no longer around our other mutual friends with whom we had gathered). His late-night "confession" was one of the most vivid memories I have of my time in Amway. This said, while being both an academic researcher and distributor helped me gain some insight, I often wonder to what degree my training impeded me from becoming as fully immersed into my distributor role as I would have liked.

Linking family/friends with distributing roles, by contrast, gave me deeper insights into distributing. The linkages between these roles showed me the two faces of distributor relationships. For example, when recruiting strangers, I learned, one is to become friends with recruits in the course of helping them to "build the business" (i.e., become successful distributors). I was also taught to become friends with other distributors in my line of sponsorship (i.e., my "family tree"). Thus, I learned that being an Amway distributor sometimes involved adding a friendship relationship onto a preexisting business relationship. I also learned that because a key source of recruits for distributors is family and friends, I sometimes needed to add business relationships to friendship or family relationships. Recruiting friends and family was difficult for me, and, as was true of some distributors, there were some friends and family that I would not risk alienating by using our relationships for business purposes. When I did take a chance and convinced a few of my graduate student friends to join me at a recruiting session, I opened myself to multiple learning opportunities.

This recruiting session was important for establishing friendships with existing distributors and for experiencing what it was like to use friendships to help build my distributorship. To begin, it was an opportunity for one of my sponsors (my brother-in-law) and his sponsor to drive from Pittsburgh to Ann Arbor to help me in a recruiting session. This time with them gave me some of the most meaningful insights into highly successful distributors. It also signaled to my upline that I was serious about being a distributor. It was during this time that my sponsor's sponsor told me, "God meant more for me than academia." He said that he did not care if I was doing a study of Amway, because once I had come to understand Amway distributing fully, I would really not want to do anything else. This experience gave me insights into the intensity of belief and the level of confidence of those who had given their hearts to the organization. It was also during this trip that my sponsors apprenticed me in many Amway recruiting techniques, such as "dream building"—finding out what people want most in life. In the process, it helped me build a bond with my sponsors' sponsor—for the business relationship to take on aspects of a friendship. Recruiting friends, by contrast, made me more acutely aware of the discomfort and vulnerability that distributors feel when trying to get friends to join. It may hurt for a stranger to reject you, but rejection from friends is especially painful.

I felt similar discomfort mixing family, distributor, and research roles. As familial relationships take on an instrumental component, it is difficult to ascertain people's motives—and anger and confusion can sometimes ensue. For example, there were times when I felt that my sister and brother-in-law were using their personal relationships with me to help them further their own businesses. However, I also felt guilty for using my family ties with them to advance my research agenda. One would think that we were "using"/depending on each other for mutual gain (a key component of distributing), but in my heart it never worked out quite that neatly. I often felt guilty about not being a good enough distributor to "repay them" adequately for all of the help that they were giving to me. I found this theme of "not working hard enough to repay the kindness of one's sponsor" to be a theme in other distributors' stories as well. The empathy I gained by the friend/family–distributor tensions led to several discussions with members about recruiting friends and family.

Taken together, the confluence of these roles (distributor–family member–friend–researcher) was one of the most difficult experiences for me in my study. These roles *did* allow me greater access. As key informants, my sister and brother-and-law helped me set up interviews. As my sponsors, they allowed me the opportunity to engage in distributing as a researcher. However, it was in the interplay of "economic" and "social" ties that I think I gained some of my deepest and most insightful glimpses into distributing. It was in this that I realized the *need* for some to become so fanatical about distributing. If you *truly believe* that you can help others by allowing them the opportunity to become a distributor, then recruiting becomes an extension of the love and caring that you have toward another person. You are then *helping* them, not using your relationship with them for economic gain. This commitment allowed some to overcome their discomfort and really build the business. Thus, this experience helped me gain occasional and powerful moments of *close and deep* access. (See this chapter's introduction for a description of *close and deep*—as well as *close and surface, distant and surface,* and *distant and deep* access.)

Exiting

I exited the organization as I entered it—in stages. First, upon finishing about a year in the field, I "left" (i.e., stopped selling and sponsoring) to write my dissertation. During this time, I kept contact with my sister and brother-in-law; after writing the dissertation, I gave a copy to them. Before reading it, they gave it to their sponsor so he could "screen it." Distributors eschew any kind of criticism of their way of life, because negative thinking (or "stinkin' thinkin'") could hinder their motivation. Initially, my sister's sponsor did not like how I depicted him. I therefore wrote him a letter of apology and offered to discuss my writings with him, but I never heard from him again. I found out only recently that he later returned my dissertation to my sister and brother-in-law and that he eventually agreed that what I had written had merit. Despite the loss of the relationship with my sponsors' sponsor, I have continued to discuss my work with my sister and brother-in-law. They continue in Amway, though not actively. I have also shared my findings with other Amway distributors—both current and former—to gain new insights into what I experienced.

Surprisingly (to me), it was not until a few years after completing my dissertation that I officially resigned as a distributor. It is not clear whether my exiting and my subsequent publications have barred the door to future interactions. However, I would likely have to rejoin if I wanted to gain close access again. If one is not "building the business," one is considered to be a "loser." But even if I chose to gain another type of access, I would likely need to build new relationships and new role linkages—and thus experience all of the cognitive, emotional, and identity implications these relationship aspects of access bring with them.

Access and Participation in a Government Agency

Clare Ginger

Between 1988 and 1994, I conducted research on the implementation of wilderness policy by the Bureau of Land Management (BLM), an agency in the Department of the Interior.[18] When I arrived in Washington, D.C., for a summer internship, I had no idea that I would eventually cross paths with rattlesnakes in the desert and hike through a stream while assisting in fish sampling. I took on the role of participant-observer for sixteen months distributed over five summers. I worked across program areas (e.g., wilderness, recreation, wildlife) in offices distributed across hierarchical levels (Washington, D.C., state, district, resource area). As I moved around the agency, I continually adapted to changing circumstances and, at times, had to prove myself. I developed "insider" status through participation in agency activities, and I balanced identities as "outside" researcher and "inside" professional. When my fieldwork was completed, the door to return to the BLM was left ajar.

Gaining Repeated Initial Access to Field Offices

After working for a summer in the Washington office, my supervisor indicated that to understand the implementation of wilderness policy, I had to go to the field. Because the BLM manages land through a hierarchy of offices in the western United States, this meant leaving Washington, D.C. By the end of the study, I had worked in nine offices located in Arizona, Utah, and Washington, D.C. With each move, I established a new basis for access, and BLM personnel made space for me, professionally and physically.

I gained access to offices across the hierarchy because my first point of access was the Washington office and because I could contribute planning, analysis, and writing skills. Unlike most BLM personnel, who enter at lower levels and work their way up, I moved down the hierarchy. At each level, while people were happy to have me contribute to their projects, they also thought I should gain experience at the next level down. Important to this dynamic was the fact that people at higher levels had authority to provide me with access to lower levels. A branch chief in Washington, D.C., could send me to state offices. Managers in state offices could send me to district and resource area offices. The reverse would not have been possible.

I do not know exactly how those in higher levels portrayed me to people in lower levels, because I was not privy to conversations in which the transactions were made. However, the dominant theme was that I would assist on projects that were under way in the office I was entering. This was not always an easy sell, and at times I had to prove myself. For example, when my supervisor in the Washington office indicated that I should go to the field, I asked to go to Utah, where wilderness policy had been controversial. By observing points of conflict, I hoped to gain insight into the difficulties of implementing policy. As I made travel plans, my supervisor informed me that a manager in Utah had indicated that I could not come. My presence and research interests became a potential point of conflict. Shortly after I arrived, the managers tried to send me back to Washington. They changed their minds once we identified tasks I could complete for them. As time passed, they came to see I did not have ill intentions.

In another case, the office that was receiving me thought that the higher level was trying to send someone who was incompetent down the line. They agreed to the arrangement only after a test period to find out whether I was a liability. In this context, I proved myself through my ability to adapt my professional skills to a range of projects. In all cases, my access to the agency and its activities deepened as I participated in both office and field projects.

Deepening Access through Participation

To deepen my access, I participated in various activities—planning and analysis tasks, site visits, and fieldwork. I experienced the work of wilderness policy implementation directly, developed a rapport with BLM employees, and became an insider. I connected with people in the agency because I worked with them. I gained access to their work (it became my work, too) and the phenomena that concerned them, land and human activities associated with it.

In each BLM office, I worked on projects with personnel located therein. In addition to participating in office work, I was invited to visit and participate in activities at field sites. For many agency personnel, experience in the BLM begins with work on the land to manage resources, such as cattle grazing allotments, mining claims, wildlife habitat, archeological sites, and recreation areas. Once they move up the hierarchy, their experience with such areas is transformed. They become visitors, often accompanied by agency personnel in lower levels of the hierarchy who have direct responsibility for field sites. My experience in going to the field began in this second way when I arrived in Utah as a visitor from Washington.

My supervisor arranged for a resource area manager to take me to visit BLM land on my first day there. We started out at 7 A.M. Soon, we were driving up a creek bed, the truck jolting over boulders at a steep incline. I acted as if this was normal. My tour guide commented that many people would be nervous. I said that I trusted his driving skills. After all, what choice did I have? We arrived at a plateau of bristlecone pines, some of the oldest trees in the world. As we looked out over the desert, he described efforts to define a wilderness boundary in the area. Later, we drove onto the forty-thousand-acre Bonneville Salt Flats. A blinding-white, icelike, seven-foot-thick field of salt surrounded us. This landscape was beyond my imagination. As we visited these and other places, we discussed various conflicts over resource use on BLM land.

This experience was instructive. It helped me understand the relevance of interacting with the land. It made me aware that such interactions can be rewarding and challenging. It also led to an insight that being in such landscapes provides a rich opportunity to learn about dilemmas that BLM employees face. Over time, agency employees offered me many similar opportunities. The land triggered stories about incidents that illustrated challenges of managing natural resources. This helped me formulate questions about how policy is applied to specific cases. It also helped me get to know people, talk open-endedly about wilderness, gather evidence about translating ideas into space, and share the experience of spectacular landscapes.

As I moved down the hierarchy, I participated in tasks that applied wilderness policy to specific areas. I learned that extreme field conditions make it difficult to manage land in some areas. In addition, ambiguous field conditions parallel a more general ambiguity that agency members face in implementing wilderness policy. However, the aesthetics of the land can provide a compelling motivation for such work. This kind of fieldwork helped me to understand more fully what BLM employees experience in translating policy to on-the-ground action.

For example, one July day a coworker and I stood at the edge of a canyon on the boundary of a wilderness study area. We wanted to see whether a trail existed across it. We scrambled over a ridge of rocks, into a dry streambed, and walked for twenty minutes. Desert rock loomed, and cholla, a plant so full of needles that it looks fuzzy, stood ready to jump into our clothes. The sun beat down, and the air was breathless, but if I was sweating, the perspiration was vaporizing. I did not think of this until later. Finding no evidence of a trail, we turned back. I took the lead and guessed correctly about where to climb out of the streambed to find our truck. I opened the door of the truck, grabbed my water bottle, and gulped down a liter. As I drank, my pores, wide open from the heat, allowed the water to pour through me. My shirt was instantly drenched. I was amazed by the desert climate and my body's reaction to it.

Coupled with such access to land was the opportunity to share in the challenges of implementing wilderness policy. Later that week, we tried to locate a wilderness boundary in a similarly arid but less topographically differentiated area. The map showed that the boundary ran along a jeep trail. On the ground we found three sets of tracks, all of which could be called jeep trails. Choosing one over another as the boundary would affect installation of a pipeline near the area. While no one expected me to take responsibility for these tasks (outdoor field skills are not my strength), people did expect that I would want to visit BLM land, that I would show respect for it, and that I had enough physical capacity not to be a liability.

Insider or Outsider?

As I gained access to and participated in the BLM, I considered issues associated with my status in the agency, which was ambiguous. Was I an inside employee or an outside researcher? My efforts to draw on professional skills to participate affected my ability to observe. My role at meetings illustrates this. At the outset, I attended meetings to observe. As I contributed work, my role shifted. At some meetings, I observed and pursued follow-up tasks. Later, I participated in and, occasionally, facilitated meetings. At this stage, going to meetings only to observe was awkward because attending meetings to which one has nothing to contribute is not normal, and not contributing when one can is also not normal. As a result, my increased role as a participant made options for detached observation less available.

In general, the ways in which I gained access as a participant in the BLM reflected an ongoing effort to balance practitioner and research identities. I had left a life as a professional in a state agency to become a graduate student. While I shifted between roles as participant and observer in the BLM, I simultaneously shifted between my practitioner and research identities.

Exiting and Ongoing Access

I entered and exited the agency several times. At the start of each summer, I came to an agreement with BLM managers about where to work. At the end of each summer, I left with an understanding that I would return. Cards, gifts, and sometimes an award accompanied my departures. My interim and final exits can be understood in terms of routines and professional choices. BLM employees routinely change positions and move from one location to another. The pattern of leaving and returning also fit with the internship program. In this program, students work for the BLM as a part of their academic plans. As I finished my Ph.D., the next step would have been to seek a permanent job in the BLM. Instead, I chose an academic path.

The door remained ajar for future access. I promised to send articles based on my work. They put me on mailing lists to receive documents. At the time of my departure, several people offered their support if I wanted to seek employment in the BLM in the future. Eight years later, I was offered a position in the agency and turned it down only after a great deal of thought and with some regret. Should I want access in the future for research, it would not be of the same nature, because my professional status has changed. An internship would not be possible. However, other arrangements are possible. In addition, because I understand how the agency is structured, I would not have difficulty in developing a basis for a new round of access.

Notes

1. Patricia Adler and Peter Adler, *Membership Roles in Field Research* (Newbury Park, Calif.: Sage, 1987), 67.

2. See J. M. Bartunek, "Changing Interpretive Schemes and Organizational Restructuring: The Example of a Religious Order." *Administrative Science Quarterly* 29 (September 1984): 355–72, and Susan Krieger, *The Mirror Dance: Identity in a Women's Community* (Philadelphia: Temple University Press, 1983).

3. Adler and Adler, "Membership Roles in Field Research," 68.

4. Carlos Casteneda is, perhaps, the best known of these converts. Casteneda, *The Teachings of Don Juan: A Yaqui Way of Knowledge* (New York: Simon and Schuster, 1968).

5. Adler and Adler, "Membership Roles in Field Research," 70.

6. See Barbara Ehrenreich, *Nickel and Dimed: On (Not) Getting By in America* (New York: Holt, 2001); and Tsuda, "Ethnicity and the Anthropologist."

7. See Ann Cornelisen, *Women of the Shadows* (Boston: Little, Brown, 1976).

8. Michael W. Coy, "Being What We Pretend to Be: The Usefulness of Apprenticeship as a Field Method," in *Apprenticeship: From Theory to Method and Back Again*, ed. Michael Coy (Albany: State University of New York Press, 1989), 110.

9. M. G. Pratt, *Different Dimensions of Access*, unpublished manuscript, University of Illinois, 1992.

10. Alex Stewart, *The Ethnographer's Method* (Thousand Oaks, Calif.: Sage, 1988); Coy, "Being What We Pretend to Be"; Jean Lave and Etienne Wenger, *Situated Learning: Legitimate Peripheral Participation* (Cambridge: Cambridge University Press, 1991).

11. Lave and Wenger, *Situated Learning*, 49.

12. Several of his ethnographic studies as well as reflections on his career choice can be found in *Turning Words, Spinning Worlds*.

13. All names are pseudonyms.

14. In each case, I let my coworkers know that in the course of my job responsibilities, I was also collecting data for my dissertation.

15. The working title of the dissertation is currently "Situating Memory: Presentations and Representations in a High Tech R&D Organization."

16. This research culminated almost ten years later in *Order without Design: Information Production and Policy Making* (Stanford, Calif.: Stanford University Press, 1989).

17. See the following for additional information about Amway and this research: M. G. Pratt, "The Happiest, Most Dissatisfied People on Earth: Ambivalence and Commitment among Amway Distributors," Ph.D. diss., University of Michigan, 1995; M. G. Pratt and C. K. Barnett, "Emotions and Unlearning in Amway Recruiting Techniques: Promoting Change through 'Safe' Ambivalence," *Management Learning* 28, no. 1 (1997): 65–88; M. G. Pratt, "The Good, the Bad, and the Ambivalent: Managing Identification among Amway Distributors," *Administrative Science Quarterly* 45 (2000): 456–93; and M. G. Pratt, "Building an Ideological Fortress: The Role of Spirituality, Encapsulation, and Sensemaking," *Studies in Cultures, Organizations, and Societies* 6 (2000): 35–69.

18. C. Ginger, "Interpreting Roads in Roadless Areas: Ambiguity, Organizational Culture, and Bureaucratic Responses to Policy Mandates," *Administration and Society* 29, no. 6 (January 1998): 723–57.

Bibliography

Adler, Patricia, and Peter Adler. *Membership Roles in Field Research*. Newbury Park, Calif.: Sage, 1987.

Agar, Michael. *The Professional Stranger: An Informal Introduction to Ethnography*. Orlando, Fla.: Academic Press, 1980.

Barber, Bernard. "The Ethics of the Use of Human Subjects in Biomedical Research (The Prototype Case)." In *Effective Social Science: Eight Cases in Economics, Political Science, and Sociology*, ed. Bernard Barber. New York: Russell Sage Foundation, 1987.

Bartunek, J. M. "Changing Interpretive Schemes and Organizational Restructuring: The Example of a Religious Order." *Administrative Science Quarterly* 29 (September 1984): 355–72.

Bell, Jeannine. *Policing Hatred: Law Enforcement, Civil Rights, and Hate Crime*. New York: New York University Press, 2002.

Berger, Michele. "Dealing with Difficult Gatekeepers, Vulnerable Populations, and 'Hooks' That Go Awry: An Access Vignette." In *Gaining Access: A Practical and Theoretical Guide for Field Researchers*, ed. Martha Feldman, Jeannine Bell, and Michele Berger. Walnut Creek, Calif.: AltaMira, 2003.

——. "Workable Sisterhood: A Study of the Political Participation of Stigmatized Women with HIV/AIDS." Ph.D. diss., University of Michigan, 1998.

Berger, Michele Tracy. "Advocates, Activists and Helpers: Multiple Expressions of Activism by HIV-Positive African-American Women in Detroit." *Womanist Theory and Research: A Journal of Womanist and Feminist of Color Scholarship and Art*, 3 (2001/2002): 21–28.

——. "'Quit Stigmatizing Us': The Role of Stigma in the Process of Political Participation among African-American Women with HIV/AIDS." In *African-American Women in Politics: A Reader*, ed. Rose Harris. Unpublished manuscript.

Bhavnani, Kum-Kum, and Angela Davis, eds. *Women in Prison: Researching Race in Three National Contexts*. New York: New York University Press, 2000.

Bolles, Richard Nelson. *What Color Is Your Parachute? A Practical Manual for Job-Hunters and Career-Changers*. Berkeley, Calif.: Ten Speed Press, 1999.

Brooks, JoAnn. "Situating Memory: Presentations and Representations in a High Tech R&D Organization." Ph.D. diss., University of Michigan.

Brown, Colin, Pierre Guillet de Monthoux, and Arthur McCullough. *The Access-Casebook.* Stockholm: Teknisk Högskolelitteratur I Stockholm AB, 1976.

Casteneda, Carlos. *The Teachings of Don Juan: A Yaqui Way of Knowledge.* New York: Simon & Schuster, 1968.

Cornelisen, Ann. *Women of the Shadows.* Boston: Little, Brown, 1976.

Coy, Michael W. "Being What We Pretend to Be: The Usefulness of Apprenticeship as a Field Method." In *Apprenticeship: From Theory to Method and Back Again,* ed. Michael Coy. Albany: State University of New York Press, 1989.

Creek, Julianne. "An Untold Story: Doing Funded Qualitative Research." In *Handbook of Qualitative Research,* ed. Norman K. Denzin and Yvonna S. Lincoln. Thousand Oaks, Calif.: Sage, 2001.

Crenshaw, Kimberle Williams. "Demarginalizing the Intersection of Race and Sex: A Black Feminist Critique of Anti-Discrimination Doctrine, Feminist Theory, and Antiracist Politics." In *Feminist Legal Theory: Readings in Law and Gender,* ed. Katherine T. Bartlett and Roseanne Kennedy. New York: Westview, 1991.

Czarniawska, Barbara. *A Narrative Approach to Organization Studies.* Thousand Oaks, Calif.: Sage, 1998.

Daniel-Echols, Marijata. "Mandates, Ideal, and Survival: The Politics of Poverty and the Implementation of Welfare Reform." Ph.D. diss., University of Michigan, 2001.

Debebe, Galaye, and Jane E. Dutton. "Getting through the Day: The Use of Relational Knowledge in Everyday Task Execution." Unpublished manuscript, 1999.

DeParle, Jason. "Learning Poverty Firsthand." *New York Times,* 27 April 1997, 32–37.

DiIulio, John, Jr. *Governing Prisons: A Comparative Study of Correctional Management.* New York: Free Press, 1987.

Dunn, Cynthia McGuire, and Gary Chadwick. *Protecting Study Volunteers in Research.* Boston: Center Watch, 1999.

Dutton, Jane E., Galaye Debebe, and Amy Wrzesniewski. "Being Valued and Devalued at Work: A Social Valuing Perspective on Relationship Sensemaking." Unpublished manuscript, 1999.

Eckstein, Susan. *The Poverty of Revolution: The State and the Urban Poor in Mexico.* Princeton, N.J.: Princeton University Press, 1977.

Edin, Kathryn, and Laura Lein. *Making Ends Meet.* New York: Russell Sage Foundation, 1997.

Ehrenreich, Barbara. *Nickel and Dimed: On (Not) Getting By in America.* New York: Holt, 2001.

Ellen, R. F. "Producing Data." In *Ethnographic Research: A Guide to General Conduct.* London: Academic Press, 1984.

Enomoto, Ernestine. "In-School Truancy in a Multiethnic Urban High School Examined through Organizational Lenses." Ph.D. diss., University of Michigan, 1993.

———. "Negotiating the Ethics of Care and Justice." *Educational Administration Quarterly* 33, no. 3 (August 1997): 351–70.

———. "Schools as Nested Communities: Sergiovanni's Metaphor Extended." *Urban Education* 32, no. 4 (November 1997): 512–31.

Ericson, Richard V. *Making Crime: A Study of Detective Work*. Toronto: Buttterworths, 1981.

Essed, Philomena. *Understanding Everyday Racism: An Interdisciplinary Theory*. Newbury Park, Calif.: Sage, 1991.

Feldman, Martha. *Order without Design: Information Production and Policy Making*. Stanford, Calif.: Stanford University Press, 1989.

Fenno, Richard. *Homestyle: House Members in Their Districts*. Boston: Little, Brown, 1978.

Garcia-Johnson, Ronie. "Exploring Environmentalism: U.S. Multinational Chemical Corporations in Brazil and Mexico." Ph.D. diss., MIT, 2000.

Geertz, Clifford. "Deep Play: Notes on the Balinese Cockfight." In *Interpretive Social Science: A Reader*, ed. Paul Rabinow and William Sullivan. Berkeley: University of California Press, 1979.

Ginger, C. "Interpreting Roads in Roadless Areas: Ambiguity, Organizational Culture, and Bureaucratic Responses to Policy Mandates." *Administration and Society* 29, no. 6 (January 1998): 723–57.

Glaser, James M. "The Challenge of Campaign Watching: Seven Lessons of Participant Observation Research." *PS, Political Science & Politics* 29 (September 1996): 533–37.

Glesne, Corrine, and Alan Peshkin. *Becoming Qualitative Researchers*. White Plains, N.Y.: Longman, 1992.

Hammersley, Martin, and Paul Atkinson. *Ethnography: Principles in Practice*. New York: Routledge, 1992.

Harrington, Brooke. "The Access Problem: Toward a Theory of Field Research Methods." Unpublished manuscript, Brown University, 1999.

Heffernan, Ester. *Making It in Prison: The Square, The Cool, and the Life*. New York: Wiley, 1972.

Hoffman, Joan E. "Problems of Access in the Study of Social Elites and Boards of Directors." In *Fieldwork Experience: Qualitative Approaches to Social Research*, ed. William Shaffir, Robert A. Stebbins, and Allan Turowetz. New York: St. Martin's, 1980.

Jelen, Ted G. "The Clergy and Abortion." *Review of Religious Research* 34 (1992): 132–51.

———. "Political Christianity: A Contextual Analysis." *American Journal of Political Science* 36 (August 1992): 692–714.

———. "The Political Consequences of Religious Group Attitudes." *Journal of Politics* 55 (February 1993): 178–90.

———. *The Political Mobilization of Religious Beliefs*. New York: Praeger, 1991.

———. *The Political World of the Clergy*. New York: Praeger, 1993.

———. "Politicized Group Identification: The Case of Fundamentalism." *Western Political Quarterly* 44 (1991): 33–52.

———. "Protestant Clergy as Political Leaders: Theological Limitations." *Review of Religious Research* 36 (1994): 23–42.

Judd, Charles M., Eliot R. Smith, and Louise H. Kidder. *Research Methods in Social Relations*. London: Holt, Rinehart & Winston, 1991.

Kenney, Michael. "Intelligence Games: A Comparative Analysis of the Intelligence Capabilities of the Drug Enforcement Agencies and Drug Trafficking Enterprises." *International Journal of Intelligence and Counter Intelligence* (Summer 2003), in press.

———. "When Organizations Out-Smart the State: Understanding the Learning Capacity of Colombian Drug Trafficking Organizations." *Transnational Organized Crime* 5, no. I (Spring 1999): 97–119.

Kleinman, Sherryl. "Learning the Ropes as Fieldwork Analysis." In *Fieldwork Experience: Qualitative Approaches to Social Research*, ed. William Shaffier, Robert A. Stebbins, and Allan Turowetz. New York: St. Martin's, 1980.

Krieger, Susan. *The Mirror Dance: Identity in a Women's Community*. Philadelphia: Temple University Press, 1983.

Lave, Jean, and Etienne Wenger. *Situated Learning: Legitimate Peripheral Participation*. Cambridge: Cambridge University Press, 1991.

Liebow, Elliot. *Tally's Corner: A Study of Negro Streetcorner Men*. Boston: Little, Brown, 1967.

Lin, Ann Chih. *Reform in the Making: The Implementation of Social Policy in Prison*. Princeton, N.J.: Princeton University Press, 2000.

Lin, Ann Chih, Amaney Jamal, and Abigail J. Stewart. "Patriarchy, Connection, and Individualism: Immigration and the Experience of Gender in Arab Immigrant Families." Unpublished manuscript.

Lofland, John, and Lyn Lofland. *Analyzing Social Settings*. Belmont, Calif.: Wadsworth, 1995.

Luker, Kristin. *Abortion and the Politics of Motherhood*. Berkeley: University of California Press, 1984.

Manion, Melanie. *Retirement of Revolutionaries in China: Public Policies, Social Norms, Private Interests*. Princeton, N.J.: Princeton University Press, 1993.

Maxwell, J. A. *Qualitative Research Design: An Interactive Approach*. Thousand Oaks, Calif.: Sage, 1996.

McCall, George, and J. L. Simmons. *Issues in Participant Observation*. London: Addison-Wesley, 1969.

McCall, Michael. "Who and Where Are the Artists?" In *Fieldwork Experience, Qualitative Approaches to Social Research*, ed. William B. Shaffier, Robert A. Stebbins, and Allan Turowetz. New York: St. Martin's, 1980.

Merry, Sally Engle. *Getting Justice and Getting Even*. Chicago: University of Chicago Press, 1990.

Meyers, Charles T. "Teaching States How to Govern: The World Bank and Governance in the 1990s." Ph.D. diss., University of Michigan.

Miller-Adams, Michelle. *The World Bank: New Agendas in a Changing World*. London: Routledge, 1999.

"New IRB Tackles Re-reviews." *Johns Hopkins Public Health* (Fall 2001).

Office for Human Research Protections. Available: ohrp.osophs.dhhs.gov.

Pepinsky, Howard. "A Sociologist on Police Patrol." In *Fieldwork Experience: Qualitative Approaches to Social Research*, ed. William Shaffier, Robert A. Stebbins, and Allan Turowetz. New York: St. Martin's, 1980.

Perlow, Leslie. "Time to Coordinate: Towards an Understanding of Work Time Standards and Norms in a Multi-Country Study of Software Engineers." *Work and Occupations* 28 (February 2001): 91–113.

Perlow, Leslie, and Jody Hoffer-Gittell. "Dynamic Alignment: The Relationship between Structures and Emergent Networks." Unpublished manuscript.

Perlow, Leslie, and John Weeks. "Who's Helping Whom: Layers of Culture and Workplace Behavior." *Journal of Organizational Behavior* 23 (2002): 235–61.

Perry, H. W. *Deciding to Decide: Agenda Setting in the United States Supreme Court.* Cambridge, Mass.: Harvard University Press, 1991.

Peshkin, Alan. A. *The Color of Strangers, the Color of Friends: The Play of Ethnicity in School and Community.* Chicago: University of Chicago Press, 1991.

Pickering, Paula. "The Choices Minorities Make about Diversity: Migration and Negotiation in Postwar Bosnia-Hercegovina." Ph.D. diss., University of Michigan, 2001.

———. "Strategies Minorities Use to Negotiate with the Majority in Post-War Bosnia-Herzegovina." In *New Approaches to Balkan Studies,* ed. Dimitris Keridis. New York: Brasseys, 2001.

Pratt, M. G. "Building an Ideological Fortress: The Role of Spirituality, Encapsulation, and Sensemaking." *Studies in Cultures, Organizations, and Societies* 6 (2000): 35–69.

———. "Different Dimensions of Access." Unpublished manuscript, University of Illinois, 1992.

———. "The Good, the Bad, and the Ambivalent: Managing Identification among Amway Distributors." *Administrative Science Quarterly* 45 (2000): 456–93.

———. "The Happiest, Most Dissatisfied People on Earth: Ambivalence and Commitment among Amway Distributors." Ph.D. diss., University of Michigan, 1995.

Pratt, M. G., and C. K. Barnett. "Emotions and Unlearning in Amway Recruiting Techniques: Promoting Change through 'Safe' Ambivalence." *Management Learning* 28, no. 1 (1997): 65–88.

"Protecting Human Beings: Institutional Review Boards and Social Science Research." *The Academe* (May–June 2001).

Prus, Robert. "Sociologist as Hustler: The Dynamics of Acquiring Information." In *Fieldwork Experience Qualitative Approaches to Social Research,* ed. William B. Shaffir, Robert A. Stebbins, and Allan Turowetz. New York: St. Martin's, 1980.

Rieder, Jonathan. *Canarsie: The Jews and Italians of Brooklyn against Liberalism.* Cambridge, Mass.: Harvard University Press, 1985.

Rose, Dan. *Black American Street Life: South Philadelphia, 1969–1971.* Philadelphia: University of Pennsylvania Press, 1987.

Rosen, Michael. *Turning Words, Spinning Worlds.* Singapore: Harwood Academic Publishers, 2000.

Sandfort, Jodi R. "Exploring the Structuration of Technology within Human Service Organizations." *Administration & Society* 34 (January 2003): 605–31.

———. "Moving beyond Discretion and Outcomes: Examining Public Management from the Front-Lines of the Welfare System." *Journal of Public Administration Research and Theory* (October 2000): 729–56.

———. "Peering into the 'Black Box': A Study of the Front-Line Organizations Implementing Welfare Policy in Michigan." Ph.D. diss., University of Michigan, 1997.

———. "The Structural Impediments to Front-line Human Service Collaboration: Examining Welfare Reform at the Front-Lines." *Social Service Review* 73, no. 3 (September 1999): 314–39.

Sandfort, Jodi R., Ariel Kalil, and Julie Gottschalk. "The Mirror Has Two Faces: Welfare Clients and Front-line Workers View Policy Reform." *Journal of Poverty* 3, no. 3 (Summer 1999): 71–91.

Schenk-Sandbergen, Loes. "Gender in Field Research: Experiences in India." In *Anthropological Journeys: Reflections on Fieldwork*, ed. Meenakshi Thapan. New Delhi: Orient Longman, 1998.

Schermer, Brian. "Architectural Communities of Practice: A Preliminary Investigation of a Source of Professional Identity." *Constructing Identity: Proceedings of the 86th ACSA Annual Meeting & Technology Conference, Association of Collegiate Schools of Architecture* (1998): 684–89.

Shaffier, William, Robert A. Stebbin, and Allan Turowetz, eds. *Fieldwork Experience: Qualitative Approaches to Social Research.* New York: St. Martin's, 1980.

Sieber, Joan. *Planning Ethically Responsible Research.* Newbury Park, Calif.: Sage, 1992.

Skolnick, Jerome. *Justice without Trial.* New York: Wiley, 1962.

Spector, Malcolm. "Learning to Study Public Figures." In *Fieldwork Experience, Qualitative Approaches to Social Research*, ed. William B. Shaffier, Robert A. Stebbins, and Allan Turowetz. New York: St. Martin's, 1980.

Spradley, James. *The Ethnographic Interview.* Fort Worth, Tex.: Holt, Rinehart & Winston, 1979.

Stack, Carol B. *All Our Kin: Strategies for Survival in a Black Community.* New York: Harper & Row, 1974.

Stewart, Alex. *The Ethnographer's Method.* Thousand Oaks, Calif.: Sage, 1988.

Stoller, Paul. *The Taste of Ethnographic Things: The Senses in Anthropology.* Philadelphia: University of Pennsylvania Press, 1989.

Terkel, Studs. *Working.* New York: Ballantine, 1972.

Tsuda, Takeyuki. "Ethnicity and the Anthropologist: Negotiating Identities in the Field." *Anthropological Quarterly* 71, no. 3 (July 1998): 878–90.

Twine, Frances Winddance. "Racial Ideologies and Racial Methodologies." In *Racing Research/Researching Race: Methodological Dilemmas in Critical Race Studies*, ed. Frances Winddance Twine and Jonathan Warren. New York: New York University Press, 2000.

Twine, Frances Winddance, and Jonathan Warren, eds. *Racing Research/Researching Race: Methodological Dilemmas in Critical Race Studies.* New York: New York University Press, 2000.

Wax, Murray. "Some Issues and Sources on Ethics in Anthropology." In *Handbook on Ethical Issues in Anthropology*, ed. Joan Cassell and Sue-Ellen Jacobs. Arlington, Va.: American Anthropological Association, 1987.

Wax, Rosalie. *Doing Fieldwork: Warnings and Advice.* Chicago: University of Chicago Press, 1973.

West, W. Gordon. "Access to Adolescent Deviants." In *Fieldwork Experience: Qualitative Approaches to Social Research*, ed. William Shaffier, Robert A. Stebbins, and Allan Turowetz. New York: St. Martin's, 1980.

Whyte, William Foote. *Street Corner Society.* Chicago: University of Chicago Press, 1943.

Wrzesniewski, Amy, and Jane E. Dutton. "Crafting a Job: Revisioning Employees as Active Crafters of Their Work." *Academy of Management Review* 26, no. 2 (2001): 179–201.

Index

About the Contributors

Martha S. Feldman earned a Ph.D. in political science at Stanford University in 1983. She is currently a professor of political science and public policy and the associate dean of the Ford School of Public Policy at the University of Michigan. Her research is in the areas of organizational theory, including the study of decision making, organizational routines and organizational culture, public management, and interpretive research methods. She is the author of articles and books, including *Order without Design: Information Production and Policy Making* (Stanford University Press, 1989) and *Strategies for Interpreting Qualitative Data* (Sage, 1995); and coauthor (with W. Lance Bennett) of *Reconstructing Reality in the Courtroom* (Rutgers University Press, 1981); (with James G. March) of "Information as Signal and Symbol in Organizations" (1981); and (with Anne M. Khademain) of "Principles for Public Management Practice: From Dichotomies to Interdependence" (2001).

Jeannine Bell received a J.D. from the University of Michigan Law School in 1999 and a Ph.D. in political science from the University Michigan in 2000. She is currently an associate professor of law at the Indiana University School of Law (Bloomington). Her research explores the enforcement of civil rights law and criminal law. She is the author of *Policing Hatred: Police Officers, Civil Rights and Hate Crime* (New York University Press, 2002). She has also published articles on the Family and Medical Leave Act and on the legal response to hate crimes.

Michele Tracy Berger earned a Ph.D. in political science at the University of Michigan in 1998. She is currently an assistant professor in the Curriculum in Women's Studies Program at the University of North Carolina, Chapel Hill. Her research interests include AIDS activism, sex work, and health policy. She is writing a book based on an ethnographic study about the lives of stigmatized women (former drug users and sex workers) with HIV/AIDS who became politically active in Detroit.

JoAnn Brooks, is a Ph.D. candidate (ABD) in public policy at the University of Michigan.

Marijata Daniel-Echols earned her Ph.D. in political science at the University of Michigan in 2001. She is currently a research associate at the High Scope Educational Research Foundation, Ypsilanti, Michigan.

Gelaye Debebe received her doctorate in organizational behavior from the University of Michigan in 2002. She is now a research associate at the Simmons Graduate School of Management.

Jane Dutton received her Ph.D. in organizational behavior in 1983 from Northwestern University. She is now the William Russell Kelly Professor of Business Administration and a professor of psychology, University of Michigan.

Ernestine Enomoto earned her Ed.D. at the University of Michigan in 1993. She is currently an associate professor in the Department of Educational Administration at the University of Hawaii at Manoa.

Clare Ginger received her Ph.D. in 1995 in urban, technological, and environmental planning from the University of Michigan. She is currently an associate professor in the School of Natural Resources, University of Vermont.

Ronie Garcia-Johnson earned her doctoral degree in political science at the University of Michigan in 1998. She is now an assistant professor of environmental policy at the Nicholas School of the Environment, Duke University.

Ted Jelen, who received his Ph.D. in political science from Ohio State University in 1979, is a professor in and chair of the Department of Political Science, University of Nevada, Las Vegas.

Amaney Jamal earned a Ph.D. in political science from the University of Michigan in 2002. Currently she is an assistant professor of political science at Columbia University.

Ann Chih Lin received her doctorate in political science in 1994 at the University of Chicago. She is an associate professor of public policy at the University of Michigan.

Melanie Manion received her Ph.D. in political science at the University of Michigan in 1989. She is an associate professor of political science and public affairs, University of Wisconsin at Madison.

Michelle Miller-Adams received her Ph.D. in 1997 in political science from Columbia University. She is currently a visiting assistant professor at Kalamazoo College.

Charles Myers, J.D. (University of Michigan, 1976) and Ph.D. (political science, University of Michigan, 2002), is the editor of *Political Science, Law, and Classics*, Princeton University Press.

Leslie Perlow earned her Ph.D. in organizational behavior at the Sloan School of Management, Massachusetts Institute of Technology, in 1995. She is an associate professor at the Harvard Business School, Harvard University.

Paula Pickering received her doctorate in political science, University of Michigan, 2001. She is an assistant professor in the Department of Government, College of William and Mary, Williamsburg, Virginia.

Michael G. Pratt received his Ph.D. in organizational psychology at the University of Michigan in 1994. He is an associate professor of business administration at the University of Illinois at Urbana.

Jodi Sandfort received her Ph.D. in political science and social work from the University of Michigan in 1997. She is a program officer at the McKnight Foundation and an associate professor at the Humphrey Institute of Public Affairs, University of Minnesota.

Brian Schermer, AIA, Ph.D. (architecture, University of Michigan, 2002), is an assistant professor of architecture in the School of Architecture and Urban Planning, University of Wisconsin at Milwaukee.

Amy Wrzesniewski received her Ph.D. in psychology from the University of Michigan in 1999. She is an assistant professor of management and organizational behavior at the Stern School, New York University.